Hors d'Oeuvre
and Canapés

By the same author . . .

COOK IT OUTDOORS

FOWL AND GAME COOKERY

THE FIRESIDE COOKBOOK

THE JAMES BEARD COOKBOOK

JAMES BEARD'S FISH COOKERY

THE COMPLETE BOOK OF BARBECUE AND ROTISSERIE
COOKING

THE COMPLETE BOOK FOR ENTERTAINING

JIM BEARD'S NEW BARBECUE COOKBOOK

JAMES BEARD'S TREASURY OF OUTDOOR COOKING

DELIGHTS AND PREJUDICES

HOW TO EAT BETTER FOR LESS MONEY (WITH SAM
AARON)

PARIS CUISINE (WITH ALEXANDER WATT)

THE COMPLETE BOOK OF OUTDOOR COOKERY (WITH
HELEN EVANS BROWN)

JAMES BEARD'S MENUS FOR ENTERTAINING

HOW TO EAT (AND DRINK) YOUR WAY THROUGH A
FRENCH (OR ITALIAN) MENU

JAMES BEARD'S AMERICAN COOKERY

BEARD ON BREAD

BEARD ON FOOD

JAMES BEARD'S NEW FISH COOKERY

JAMES BEARD'S THEORY AND PRACTICE OF GOOD
COOKING

NEW RECIPES FOR THE CUISINART FOOD PROCESSOR
(WITH CARL JEROME)

THE NEW JAMES BEARD

BEARD ON PASTA

Hors d'Oeuvre and Canapés

By JAMES BEARD

Quill

New York

Library of Congress Cataloging in Publication Data

Beard, James, 1903–
    Hors d'oeuvre and canapés.

    Bibliography: p.
    Includes index.
    Reprint. Originally published: New York : M. Barrows, 1963
    1.Cookery (Appetizers)   2. Cocktail parties.
I. Title.
TX740.B43   1985   641.8′12   84-22339
ISBN: 0-688-04226-0

Printed in the United States of America

2 3 4 5 6 7 8 9 10

FOREWORD

It is very gratifying to find that a book I wrote nearly forty-five years ago is still in demand. It was then a pioneering book, written in the hope of promoting intelligent and delicious food for the American cocktail hour. Now it turns out also to have been a durable basic book on the subject.

It all began, I believe, in the mid-1930s when I first met Bill Rhode and his sister Irma in New York. We had many interests in common, notably love of good food and drink. We shared many ideas and preferences—not to say prejudices—about food, and in the course of trying out our own cooking on each other and spending hours in discussion about it, we agreed we both wanted to go into the food business.

We decided the thing to do was to open a shop. The collective advice of a number of our food-loving friends—including that dedicated bon vivant Lucius Beebe—led us to settle on cocktail-party and buffet foods. There followed a long siege of experimentation with our friends serving as guinea pigs. A first objective was to eliminate all the various horrors prevalent on the routine hors d'oeuvre tray—cottony bread and sagging toast, spreads and cheeses of no identifiable flavor, multi-colored pastry-tube piping, and tidbits on toothpicks coyly stuck into a grapefruit.

We drew on classic cuisine, foreign cookery, and our own imaginations for ideas. Among our early experiments that survived to become part of the shop's repertory were tiny artichoke hearts stuffed with pâtés; sandwiches made of thin slices of meat instead of bread, with filling in between; slices of cucumber instead of bread as the bases for fillings. We used raw vegetables often, used only the finest bread when we did use it, and the most delicious fillings we could devise.

The shop caught on. We were able to expand and add to our wares buffet foods such as vichyssoise, baked hams, a homemade white fruit cake. The business flourished until the war came, and with it, rationing. Then the shop had to be sold and we went our separate ways. Bill Rhode went off to be one of the first editors of *Gourmet* magazine. He was a great character and a man of infinite charm and wit. His sister Irma later wrote several extremely good cookery books.

Those were hectic days all around, and in the midst of them I had an offer from a publisher—Barrows: Could I do a book on hors d'oeuvre and have it finished in six weeks? I had to sleep on it, but the years in the shop had served me well. I knew I had the material, and this little volume *was* delivered, on the dot, at the end of six weeks.

Although a new edition of HORS D'OEUVRE AND CANAPÉS was completely rechecked and re-edited in 1963, it remained essentially the same book. It seems to me, when I now read it carefully once again, that we had looked ahead in that shop more than we knew. What we did then, we did as pioneers in a field that has since grown unbelievably. There came, after the war, a gastronomic renaissance in which a huge public has participated. I take pride in the fact that this little book today is very much in tune with that renaissance and that it must have contributed to it.

J. B.
(1984)

INTRODUCTION TO THE
FIRST EDITION

"*Hors d'oeuvre* means 'outside the meal' and regardless of how many different sorts may be provided 'outside' or before any one meal, there is but one meal or *oeuvre,* so that, in French, *oeuvre* remains in the singular and *hors d'oeuvre* never is written *hors d'oeuvres*."—*André Simon's French Cook Book.*

"Outside the meal," or, as Mr. Webster has put it, "outside the work" (his wife must have been a bad cook) has come into our language as the appetizer. The hors d'oeuvre is a rite rather than a course and its duty is to enchant the eye, please the palate, and excite the flow of the gastric juices, if we may be so very technical, so that the meal to follow will seem doubly tempting and flavorful.

Hors d'oeuvre, or its ancestor, probably came to us from China, across the Steppes into Russia and Scandinavia, thence to France and the other Middle European countries. Perhaps it came to Italy, Greece, and the Balkans from Russia, or again through Persia. Today we have a series of national customs that are closely related: the Swedish *smörgåsbord* table, the Russian *zakuska*, the *antipasto* of Italy and the hors d'oeuvre of France.

I am quite sure the first sign of it in this country probably appeared in some roughly-hewn, pioneer bar on the California coast. Perhaps some homesick Frenchman, longing for the customs of his faraway homeland, set up a simple hors d'oeuvre tray on the bar of his ramshackle saloon. News spread around town that there was a free lunch at Frenchie's bar. Thus came the day of the five-cent beer and free lunch throughout America. The free lunch became a national institution and was probably responsible for the sale of a great deal of beer. Huge tables were laid with an amazing assortment of foods, and not party foods either but literally living up to the term "lunch." Many's the man who with a dime for a glass of beer made himself a good meal at the nearest bar. This quaint and amazing and strange custom ended with Prohibition and since Repeal there have been few attempts to revive it in the old way. We have made many changes in our drinking habits, we Americans. Women have become as numerous as men at the bars. The cocktail "lounge" has come into our lives and the free lunch has become the hors d'oeuvre.

In China and in most European countries the first course,

or the prelude to the meal, is nearly always a selection of choice tidbits which, with their savory qualities or salty tang, have a tendency to stimulate the appetite to a point that makes the succeeding courses seem much more enjoyable. We see in the *smörgåsbord* and the *zakuska*, the hors d'oeuvre table of France, and the *antipasto* the same thing carried to various degrees of elaboration: there are always many varieties of pickled, dried, and salt fish served in spicy sauces; cold meats and galantines; egg dishes; marinated vegetables and fruits; many hot dishes with highly seasoned sauces, and a wealth of other things too numerous to list here lest the book be entirely a hymn of praise to the European cooks who have created such delicacies.

One restaurant in Paris which was famous for its almost endless variety of hors d'oeuvre would, at luncheon time, serve you an entire meal of them in a most novel fashion: you were brought a complete selection of fishes, followed by meats, vegetables, eggs, fruits, all in bountiful arrangement on little wagons. Such abundance is of course impossible to the average home, but it shows the infinite number of ideas and never-ending combinations which may be called upon to make the hors d'oeuvre tray or table complete.

In America since the repeal of the Prohibition Amendment there has developed a new and, at times, delightful form of hospitality—the cocktail party. With this has come the use of the age-old French term for "outside the meal" food. But instead of huge buffets groaning with succulent morsels, as in European homes (formerly!), the age-old appetizer has become streamlined along with our trains and automobiles and living.

We have developed a most amazing variety of finger food to go with the cocktail and the glass of sherry, literally hundreds of variations, some of course borrowed from our European and Asiatic backgrounds and many that are distinctly our own. In many ways this is one of the most truly American contributions to the art of good living. It is with this finger food that I am concerned in this book and with the cocktail party, whether it be the simple "drop in for a drink" type or the great "crush" that pays a year's social debts in one fell swoop.

To the average American hostess, practically everything from a potato chip to a six-rib roast of beef comes under the term hors d'oeuvre. I am frequently asked in my shop, "What is the difference between a canapé and an hors d'oeuvre?" It is really a very frail difference, but one that should be cleared up here and now. So, I shall try to clarify the various terms that are in common use today and to list the recipes under their respective headings.

Hors d'oeuvre we have already defined as a general term, but Americans have developed what is known as the cocktail hors d'oeuvre or snack. This is a small, hasty bite served usually without bread or biscuit, sometimes on a toothpick and sometimes under its own power.

Hot hors d'oeuvre may be eaten with a fork, as they often have a heavy sauce or a marinade. These are served in endless varieties and in many combinations.

Canapé probably comes from the French word that has

come to be "canopy" in English. It means literally, and I again quote Mr. Webster, "a bed with mosquito netting." That is fairly accurate, for we have a bed of toast or biscuit or pastry shell, hidden by the "mosquito netting" of savory butters or pastes or the million and two things used these days for taste-bud stimulants.

Smörgåsbord is the Swedish cold table, beautifully appointed and laden with all sorts of fish, meat, game, salads, cheese, hot savory dishes, sweet-sour dishes, breads, fresh butter, and numberless dishes exciting to the appetite and encouraging to thirst. These are always washed down with quantities of *akavit*. Once around the usual *smörgåsbord* table ordinarily is enough, but I must confess to seeing people in Swedish restaurants in this country go around again and again and again. Lucullan moderns!

Zakuska is the Russian equivalent for this, probably with more caviar and perhaps more violent kinds of fish and much black bread and vodka.

Antipasto is the Italian variation of the theme. It is notable for its vegetables and beautiful sausages and some of the master sauces Italians create. Good olive oil and wine vinegar are aids to this splendid pre-dinner. With it vermouth finds great favor as an apéritif.

So, they all add together and reach the same answer. As is natural, the northern countries provide more body-heating foods and the southern ones the lighter, greener things. All of them are alluring to the stomach and the eye and all of them should be well washed down with the drink of your choosing.

The contrary sister of all these has a home in England and a firmly established one at that: she is *the savory* or savoury, which has never seemed to achieve a vogue in this country. A savory is really a canapé or snack served after the sweet, to kill the sweet taste and clear the way for the coffee and liqueurs. The savory may be hot or cold.

It is a far cry from the fly-specked and hearty free-lunch table of the American pioneer saloon to the perfectly appointed hors d'oeuvre table of today, but I think America has jumped the gap and is safely on the modern side. It is this modern picture I hope to present in this book.

J. B.
(1940)

CONTENTS

Foreword v

Introduction to the First Edition ix

CHAPTER 1 THE KEY TO THE COCKTAIL
PARTY 1

CHAPTER 2 COLD HORS D'OEUVRE FOR
COCKTAIL PARTIES 19
Meat Hors d'Oeuvre
Cheese Hors d'Oeuvre
Seafood Hors d'Oeuvre
Egg Hors d'Oeuvre
Vegetable Hors d'Oeuvre
Fruit Hors d'Oeuvre

CHAPTER 3   CANAPÉS   72
             Canapé Foundations
             Butters
             Spreads
             Canapés
             Canapés with *Brioche*
             Stuffed Bread Rings
             Tiny *Choux*

CHAPTER 4   COCKTAIL SANDWICHES   108
             Fillings
             The Highball Sandwich
             Sandwiches with Champagne or
                Punches
             Open-Face Sandwiches
             Hot Sandwiches
             Rolled Sandwiches

CHAPTER 5   HOT HORS D'OEUVRE FOR
             COCKTAIL PARTIES   126
             Hot Canapés
             Allumettes
             Barquettes
             Beignets, or Fritters
             Bouchées
             Croquettes
             Turnovers
             Tartlets
             Hors d'Oeuvre *en Brochette*
             Miscellaneous Hot Snacks

CHAPTER 6 ACCESSORIES 173
Nuts, Pickles, and Chips
Biscuits
Stretching the Cocktail Party
The Soft Drinks
The Tea Table

CHAPTER 7 HORS D'OEUVRE AS A FIRST
COURSE AT LUNCHEON OR
DINNER 184

CHAPTER 8 STOCKING THE LARDER 193

Index 198

Hors d'Oeuvre
and Canapés

CHAPTER 1

THE KEY TO
THE COCKTAIL PARTY

L'*origine du mot cocktail est incertaine. Vraisemblable-*
ment anglo-américaine, elle signifie "queue de coq," soit
à cause du chatoiement des mélanges de liqueurs colorées,
soit, selon certaines étymologies, parce que le cocktail
primitif des pionniers de Manhattan consistait . . . en
plumes de coq trempées dans une décoction de piment
dont ils se chatouillaient le goiser, pour les inciter à boire.
—Prosper Montagné, *Larousse Gastronomique.*

The cocktail party no longer means a bottle of gin, a can
of sardines, and a package of potato chips from the corner
grocery. It has become a definite part of the entertainment
schedule for every household, large and small. To the one-
room apartment dweller, it is the solution for extending

hospitality in the limits of his domain; and to the owner of the great house, it is the fat check for paying old social debts. It is an institution, and a gay one; one that brings forth the best, and sometimes the worst, in all of us. I look upon it as the twentieth-century salon.

Whether there are three or four guests casually asked to drop in on their way home from work, or three hundred who answer the bidding of an elaborately engraved card, the rules are the same. The major ones are: a hospitable and, to say the least, fairly sober host; good liquor and well-mixed, nay, perfectly mixed drinks; food good-looking enough to pique the appetite and delicious enough to continue it.

Trusting this will not sound like an etiquette book, I shall lay down not only a series of "Do's" but also a series of "Don't's," for this function. Here they are:

DON'T invite more people than your living room will hold, and don't keep adding to the list, one here and one there. If your place is small, give a series of parties and make out a list for each and adhere to it. It is disastrous to prepare for ten, have thirty arrive, and remember your folly too late.

If you are fond of your friends, don't make guinea pigs of them. The time to try out new drinks is when you are alone or with some kind and understanding friend.

Unless you have a completely equipped bar, don't try to serve (beyond the usual whiskies) more than two types of mixed cocktails plus, perhaps, a wine or apéritif and a soft drink at any one party. And above all, don't try to force liquor on your guests. Many people, for reasons of their own, will not or cannot touch alcohol but want to come to your party for yourself. Give such guests some sort of appetizing potion, prepared with as much care and love as the cocktail. (I list these later.)

DON'T be the type of host who has to be put to bed by the guests. *You* are doing the entertaining, and you are there to see that your guests have a good time. Unless you have an unheard-of capacity you will find it difficult to have a drink with everyone and still be charming and thoughtful to the late arrivals. There is plenty of time after the crush is over to catch up with the hangers on, and there are always plenty of them—I am usually one myself.

DON'T forget that the food at this party is as important as the drinks. And don't forget, something tucked away somewhere to sup on after the party rounds out the evening for you and the friends who simply will not go. (More on this later, too.) Don't be too lavish and don't be too mean as the party progresses. If you shoot the works for the five-o'clock guests and starve the seven-o'clock arrivals, you have failed miserably as a host.

DON'T forget, the cocktail party is a festive event; make your house show it. Flowers and light and warmth of welcome are as important as food and drink.

Do know how many are coming and do know that they are congenial. Remember the Montagues and the Capulets and judge accordingly.

Do have plenty of food and drink, for one complements the other and both make for good fellowship and pleasant living.

Do remember to see that the guests are well cared for. One cannot be a good host and be mixing drinks, washing glasses, replenishing trays, and talking to guests all at the same time. The neighborliness of America often permits the loan of someone's Susie or Bertha or William for the afternoon. It is not "swank" to have ample service; it is the secret of relaxed and casual entertaining. And excellent men and women who go about serving such parties are available nowadays in any city or town. Some of them are marvels at making appetizers and mixing drinks as well as looking like well-trained servants when the party is on. Always be sure that whoever tends bar knows what he is about, else in that lack lies your downfall. And incidentally, don't forget that these itinerant retainers are specialists in their line and deserve great consideration and pleasant treatment. A job well done deserves a bonus.

Do plan ahead so that from the minute the first guest arrives till the last one leaves there is a spirit of relaxed gaiety that infects everyone who enters your door. The cocktail party is not a formal affair; it is as democratic as the subway and its informality should be the keynote.

Do remember these things and plan accordingly: that one should plan on hard liquor, plus a cocktail sherry, apéritif, or Madeira, and a soft drink; and have sufficient quantities—none of it can spoil. The standard cocktails are best: Martinis, Manhattans, Old Fashioneds, Daiquiris.

Of course, in summer and at the holiday season, you may want to serve some sort of flowing bowl which is a specialty of the house, but stay away from the other weird concoctions which may appeal to you but are poison to Cousin Bill and a good many other people, too.

Never serve the champagne cocktail—that horror! Good vintage champagne is a treat in itself and should never be ruined by the addition of bitters and sugar and "fruit salad." Champagne punches are another story; but if you have good champagne—and who would serve anything else to his guests?—serve it well cooled and in its virgin state!

For the simple party, it is enough to have one cocktail, a Martini, for instance, and perhaps a Scotch-and-soda and a sherry if anyone wants it. If you serve dry sherry, see that it is slightly cooled, for that brings out the luscious qualities of the grape.

For the great crush of two hundred or so, you will have enough service to offer a selection of six or seven different drinks: a choice of four cocktails, Scotch and Bourbon and soda, a sherry and a Madeira. In addition, and preferably in another room if possible, there should be a well-appointed, completely stocked tea table for the benefit of those, and they are many, who still prefer a cup of tea and a sandwich to any cocktail in the world. Be sure to have your most decorative and charming guest presiding at the tea table.

If the party is simply three or four old friends gathering around the fire in the late afternoon, a bottle of sherry or a bottle of fine champagne is delightful.

For any party, average four drinks per person—some may take eight and some may sip one for three hours; and have a reserve hidden in your wine cellar whether this "cellar" is the hall closet or the huge, honeycombed cellars of a great house.

Have oceans of ice; don't depend entirely on the electric refrigerator. If you have a great number of guests, order extra tubs of cubes from your local ice company. In many cities there are services which will provide several dozen cubes in packages, delivered to order.

While there are still people who insist on putting ashes and cigarette butts into their cocktail glasses, and throwing butts across the room into the fireplace to test their marksmanship, the great majority want ash trays, plenty of them and roomy ones. These must be emptied with some degree of regularity all afternoon, by a servant who has been so instructed, or the mess and the stench will be overpowering.

Have plenty of cigarettes, and not only your own brand.

Be sure to see that the glass situation is well in hand, for it is difficult to keep up a steady washing in the kitchen and keep the steady pace of service out front. It is simple these days, with the five-and-dimes and the department stores offering attractive glasses for very little money, to have a supply of auxiliaries which can go to the top shelf between parties. In a small community where a great deal of entertaining goes on, a community set may be acquired which can be sent around from house to house. In any city where there are catering services all kinds of glasses may be rented for a very nominal sum.

Plenty of food is as important at such a party as plenty of liquor, and both should be of the highest quality. The food, no matter how simple, should show some degree of imagination; for remember, you are paying a compliment in food and drink and nothing but the best is good enough for friends. You know your guests' capacities, but five pieces per person is a minimum. From there on, let your own ideas guide you. I have seen tables sagging with food remain untouched and, too, I have known the time when all sorts of emergency tactics had to be employed to feed guests who were seemingly on the verge of starvation.

Hors d'oeuvre are the most elastic of food, for they may fit into any style of service. You may have great trays of them passed with regularity by the butler or maid; or they may be placed on plates or trays and left on a serving table for guests to help themselves. Again, for the really big party, there may be a huge buffet table which simply groans with the prize products of your kitchen and brain.

I visit a simple home in New York where hospitality reigns with as friendly a hand as anywhere I have ever known. With our simple drinks in front of the fire, there is always a tray with a choice morsel of cheese, perhaps, and some anchovies fresh from the can or bottle, some fresh, green, crisp tidbit such as the first green onions of the season, or a bit of succulent fennel, or some superb celery. With this, some crisp biscuits and an invitation to help oneself. Each morsel is delicious and stimulating to the appetite, for it is flavored with good will and love and understanding. (Incidentally, remember that in speaking of biscuits I mean what in America are generally called crackers. The English term "biscuit" happens now to be more or less frequently used because most of the cocktail biscuits which have become popular formerly were imported; so, from now on, when I say biscuit, I don't mean the baking-powder variety.)

In contrast to this hospitable spot in New York, I recall a most formal spot in California where every door knob and every cocktail glass was a museum piece. Here, when bidden for cocktails, I was confronted with a table that had graced the palace of some now-forgotten doge, and found huge joints of beef and perfectly done birds and the choicest delicacies the market afforded and the finest of cheeses and sauces. But here, amidst all the perfect appointments, there was a lack of hospitality so apparent to everyone that a heavy hush hung over the party. There was a definite feeling that the party was a duty to you and that you were being repaid for something you had extended in your own strange and peculiar way. In this setting, with some of the charm of that tiny New York apartment, a party could have been a thing such as dreams are made of. So, season well anything you do with the boon of love and hospitality and you need have no fears for the success of the affair.

While this book is not primarily a cocktail book, there are certain things to remember about drinks and certain basic recipes and ideas which will help in preparing drinks and furnishing the bar.

First as to glassware. Simple, well-designed glassware is always preferred. America has so much that is fine nowadays that a choice should not be at all difficult. You will want to choose the three-ounce, stemmed cocktail glass which serves for practically ever sort of cocktail; the seven-ounce Old Fashioned glass that has a good flare and a firm base; and the delicate, two-ounce sherry glass of graceful design. In considering highball glasses, and herein lies a battle, there are many schools of thought. Some prefer the ten-ounce glass which requires perhaps an ounce and a quarter of whiskey, others the twelve-ounce glass requiring an ounce and a half, and still others the fourteen-ounce glass with a full two ounces of whiskey to a highball. Personally, I cast my vote for the twelve or fourteen, preferably the latter, for it is a more functional glass. It may be used for the highball, the Tom Collins or rum Collins, summer punches, and even for a mint julep if you have the courage to make this drink.

Choose glasses of standard quality and design with a minimum of decoration. I prefer a clear glass, but that is a matter of personal preference. If colored glass is your choice, you should have it; to me the drink supplies the color and is enhanced by the gleaming crystal. Also, choose with regard to your pocketbook; however, the best is never expensive, for it is something that is a part of the decorative scheme of the home and something bought to last and to complement other things in your decorative idea.

Glass cocktail shakers, and mixers for Martinis and Manhattans (these never should be shaken), are greatly to be desired, as they give you a chance to see what you are doing and can be kept spotlessly clean. Large shakers are economical, for they are equally efficient for few or many cocktails.

You will find a glass jigger useful but, personally, I prefer a chemist's measuring glass because it is larger and on the whole more accurate. After all, each time you mix a cocktail it is just as important to be accurate as it is when mixing a chemical formula and the chemist's glass serves as a gentle reminder.

Other bits of hardware you will find necessary are a good strainer, one of the professional type which fits into a mixer and drains every drop of the precious fluid leaving the ice behind; a mixing spoon with a long handle; a good, heavy muddler; glass muddlers or spoons (after dinner coffees are the best) for your Old Fashioned-drinking guests; the efficient and useful squeezer used in most bars—it can squeeze a lime within an inch of its existence.

If you take pride in bartending, you will take care never to run out of ice. You will find the big vacuum ice buckets a boon. Find one of lavish size, for plenty of ice is the first requisite of good drinking in this country.

And don't forget to have the most efficient corkscrews and bottle openers, and the patented beer-can openers for your beer-drinking guests.

Beware of too many gadgets on your bar or mixing table, for they get in the way and sooner or later are bound to confound and muddle you. Have good equipment and be sure it is functional.

If you have no bar in your home, choose a steady table of good size and set your things on it. A good-looking cloth that is meant for that table and that alone, is something you need. If it is possible to store one of those portable bars, a boon to the small-apartment dweller, do so, for such a bar has éclat and is a most efficient piece of equipment. It has ample room for bottles and glasses and the ice bucket and tongs and will hold a few other items here and there.

If you are serving champagne, don't forget to provide plenty of ice buckets or champagne coolers, for champagne without the proper coolth is dull stuff indeed—as it is also when it is too cold.

Trays, deep ones, for glasses are a boon. If you will scour the hardware stores for the heavy, French lacquered tin baking pans that have a depth of about two and a half inches and large, firm handles, you will find they make excellent cocktail trays. Even the tipsy guest who becomes helpful usually can manipulate one of these without doing too much damage.

Linens are important for the cocktail party. If there is a buffet table, you will want your most exquisite linen or lace cloth on your gayest peasant cloth as a background for the appetizing morsels on display. I vote, too, for the linen cocktail napkin which has body and absorbent qualities never found in paper. It is a compliment and a nice one to be particular enough to want to offer the best of everything to your guest.

China and silver, too, play an important part in the scheme for the cocktail party, for many people prefer a plate and fork service, and there are certain things which really require the aid of a fork. For these there are no set rules, though generally a bread-and-butter plate or salad size are the most desirable. Or you may have some of the amusing wooden plates so much in vogue lately, or your Great Aunt Abigail may have sent you a dozen silver plates for a wedding present. At any rate, you may use practically anything you have from glass to wood and feel that you're doing the right thing. Salad forks or desert size are best for hors d'oeuvre service.

Hot hors d'oeuvre need hot serving plates. If you are fortunate enough to have hot-water dishes similar to the English buffet dishes, fine; but if you haven't, make the best of it by having everything doubly hot. Plenty of scalding hot water into which to dip plates for hot foods will solve your problem.

Do not despair if you are short plates and silver, for it is always possible to rent these things. Any catering or personal service shop has these to rent and they usually are good looking and nominally priced.

Here are some good and truly basic recipes for cocktails and long drinks. You will find it helpful in planning your party to budget the liquor beforehand. Allow an average of thirteeen drinks per bottle and you will be safe on all sides. Of course, with vermouth and liqueurs used for flavoring, you will get far more; but for rum, whiskey, gin, brandy and applejack, thirteen drinks allows a safe margin.

THE MARTINI—*Circa 1940*

Put plenty of ice in your mixer. Add two or three strips of lemon peel; add three parts of gin and one part of French vermouth. Stir, and pour into chilled glasses with tiny cocktail onions.

THE MARTINI—*Circa 1961*

The modern Martini is made with nine parts of gin now to one of vermouth. In other words, there's just a hint of vermouth as compared with its predecessor.

THE STANDARD MANHATTAN

> *¾ Rye whiskey*
> *¼ Italian vermouth*
> *dash of Angostura bitters per drink*

Stir vigorously in the mixer with plenty of ice. The maraschino cherry is the traditional addition to this drink.

THE DRY MANHATTAN

> *¾ Rye whiskey*
> *¼ French vermouth*

Stir in the mixer with plenty of ice and serve. No cherry.

THE DAIQUIRI

> *juice of ½ a lime*
> *2-ounce jigger of Bacardi rum*
> *1 teaspoonful of super-fine sugar*

Shake well with plenty of ice and strain into iced glass.

THE BRONX (*now a curiosity*)

> *⅓ gin*
> *⅓ French and Italian vermouth*
> *⅓ orange juice*

Shake well and strain into cocktail glasses.

WHITE SATIN (*a great Prohibition cocktail*)

> *½ gin*
> *½ fresh grapefruit juice*

Shake well with plenty of ice and strain into glasses.

THE SCREWDRIVER

> *2 ounces vodka*
> *1 cup orange juice*

Put several ice cubes into a fourteen-ounce glass, pour in the vodka and orange juice, and stir languidly.

VODKATINI

> *4 parts vodka*
> *1 part French-type vermouth*

Stir with ice as with a Martini. Strain and serve with a twist of lemon peel.

OLD FASHIONED

> *1 lump of sugar*
> *1 slice of lemon peel*
> *2 dashes of Angostura bitters*
> *3 ounces of whiskey, rum or brandy*

Mash the sugar and bitters and lemon peel with a muddler. Add the ice and the spirit and stir well.

This is my own version of the Old Fashioned, for I loathe "fruit salad" in a drink and all the decorations that usually accompany this simple cocktail.

DARK RUM COCKTAIL

> *¾ Jamaica rum*
> *1 teaspoonful brown sugar for each 3 ounces rum*
> *¼ lime juice*

Shake well with plenty of ice and strain into glasses.

Tom Collins

> 1 tablespoonful of sugar syrup or bar sugar
>   juice of 1 lemon or 1½ limes
> 4 ounces of gin

Shake well in a cocktail shaker; pour into a twelve-ounce glass with plenty of ice and fill with club soda. No fruit.

The same recipe is correct for a rum Collins, using either Jamaica or Bacardi rum in place of gin.

Side car

> ⅓ lemon juice
> ⅓ Cointreau
> ⅓ Cognac

Shake well with plenty of ice and strain into glasses.

Sours (whiskey, rum or brandy)

> 2 ounces of the liquor chosen
> 1 teaspoonful of bar sugar
>   juice of 1 lemon

Shake well with plenty of ice. Strain into a four-ounce glass.

FRENCH SEVENTY-FIVES

Proceed as for Tom Collins, but substitute domestic champagne for club soda.

JACK ROSE

> ⅔ *applejack*
> ⅓ *lemon juice*
> *dash of Grenadine*

Shake well with ice; strain into glasses.

VERMOUTH CASSIS *(an ideal summer drink)*

> *4-ounce glassful of French vermouth*
> *crème de Cassis liqueur to taste*

Mix in a tall glass with ice and fill with club soda. Add a zest of lemon.

STINGER

> *2 parts Cognac*
> *1 part white crème de menthe*

Shake with cracked ice, strain into cocktail glasses.

BLOODY MARY

> 1 jigger vodka
> 1 dash Tabasco
> 1 teaspoon lemon juice
> 6 ounces tomato juice
> 1 teaspoon Worcestershire Sauce
>   salt and pepper to taste

Shake with ice and strain into a ten-ounce glass.

MY FAVORITE BLOODY MARY

> 1 jigger vodka
>   juice of ½ lemon
>   dash of Worcestershire Sauce
> 2 ounces tomato juice
>   dash of Tabasco
>   dash of salt

Shake vigorously and pour into a chilled glass.

And now, the table is set, the bottles laid out, the glasses gleaming, the flowers in their places, the cigarettes and ash trays arranged, food for the eye and the body and the soul ready. Adjust your tie or powder your nose, forget cares, let your best smile come out, and on to a gay and happy adventure.

CHAPTER 2

COLD HORS D'OEUVRE
FOR COCKTAIL PARTIES

Constant workouts with various types of appetizers
have given me a chance to try almost every type of equipment for making hors d'oeuvre and spreads and butters
and sandwiches. I feel that a few hints in that direction may
be of value to you in preparing for your guests, so here
you are:

You need plenty of sharp knives in all sizes including at
least two that may be sharpened to almost razor sharpness
so that things may be cut paper thin.

At least one set, and preferably two, of the metal tubes
or cylinders which are commonly called decorating or
pastry sets. You will find them in various shops in different

types of metal. For most women, the smaller and less expensive sets will be easier to handle. The metal cylinders are somewhat handier than cloth pastry bags.

A curved-blade hand chopper and wood chopping bowls in varying sizes, for parsley and other herbs and for hard-cooked eggs. Or else good sharp knives and your regular chopping board.

A mortar and pestle for making pastes and pulverizing.

Nowadays, an electric blender is a necessity, not a luxury.

I made a very successful rack for holding cornucopias upright with one of the open wire-mesh cake coolers, attached with small legs to a tray. Spools make admirable legs, or wire legs may be welded to the rack and to the tray for very little. Cornucopias of meat or fish will stand supported in the openings of the mesh and keep in perfect condition till they are ready to be served.

Canapé cutters, sharp ones, of all sizes and in many shapes.

Several of the ball-shaped vegetable scoops in various sizes, for they have many uses.

Shredders and graters; choose your own type.

Spatulas; they are most accommodating tools.

A pair of wooden butter paddles.

A pepper mill if you don't already have one, for freshly ground pepper improves any mixture that calls for that spice.

A salt mill to grind coarse salt. Coarse salt in cooking adds flavor, and once you use it, you will never switch back to the old, commercial type.

The following recipes for small snacks are some of my favorite bits of cold cocktail food. They are served without bread or crackers and are easily eaten with the fingers. They are decidedly decorative and may be arranged to make a most appetizing tray.

As a rule, the quantity in these recipes is for about twelve pieces.

❧MEAT HORS D'OEUVRE

DANISH HAM ROLLS

Trim the excess fat from six paper-thin slices of Parma ham or prosciutto, the delicately flavored Italian ham one may buy in almost any Italian grocery carrying smoked meats. Spread thin slices of smoked salmon over this till the ham is completely covered. Roll very tightly and cut into rolls about one inch long. Spear with toothpicks and chill before serving. A little freshly ground black pepper will do a lot to flavor the ham.

BEEF ROLLS WITH PÂTÉ

Six slices of rare roast beef one eighth inch thick; sirloin or "eye" of beef is best for this particular roll. Cut beef into strips one to one and one half inches wide and three inches long. Spread each slice with some *pâté de foie gras*

or any good liver paste. Salt to taste and roll. Secure with
toothpicks and chill before serving. The ends may be
dipped in chopped parsley before serving.

BEEF ROLLS CHINOISE

Prepare dry mustard with the syrup from preserved kumquats or with orange marmalade, using one teaspoonful
of mustard to one and one half teaspoonfuls of the syrup
or marmalade. Prepare twelve slices of beef, the rarer the
better as before; spread them very thinly with the mustard
sauce. Salt well and sprinkle a teaspoonful of chopped
chives or finely chopped onions on each. Roll tightly and
secure with a toothpick. Dip each end in a mixture of one
tablespoonful of chopped parsley and one of chopped
chives. These rolls make one of the most drink-provoking
hors d'oeuvre known to man. And, a tip—this is a real
man's snack, definitely not for a female audience. Swell
with highballs, too!

This same treatment may be given to slices of cold
smoked tongue cut to a thickness of about one sixteenth
of an inch and trimmed carefully to about one by three
inches.

TONGUE WITH ROQUEFORT

Prepare twelve tongue slices as described for the other
meats above. Spread them very lightly with Roquefort-
cheese butter (the recipe will be found in the chapter on

canapés); roll and secure with a toothpick. If you trim the edges carefully, this roll will need no garnishing, for the contrast of light and dark gives a well-tailored appearance.

TONGUE WITH ASPARAGUS NO. 1

Spread the squares of tongue with a little mayonnaise mixed with dry mustard, about one half teaspoonful of mustard to a tablespoonful of mayonnaise. Roll around an asparagus tip; trim and secure with a toothpick.

TONGUE WITH ASPARAGUS NO. 2

For this one you will need infinite patience. Cut the squares of tongue a little larger, two inches by three and one half inches. Round them out till they are uneven ovals. Use the rack I spoke about at the beginning of this chapter for making cornucopias. Take a one-inch asparagus tip and fold the base of the oval of tongue around the end of it; you may secure it with a bit of raw egg white. Place it in a wire-mesh rack in an upright position, and allow these to chill in the refrigerator for at least one and one half hours. (Season as in preceding recipe.)

BEEF WITH ANCHOVY

Beef slices are rolled around fillets of anchovy and secured with a toothpick. Roll them in chopped egg and chill before serving. Egg white will simplify the process of coating with chopped egg or parsley. Brush the rolls with white of egg and the garnish will adhere much more easily and will not have a tendency to drop off.

PIQUANT VEAL SLICES

If you have some cold roast veal, you may make a very interesting and unusual snack. Slice it very thin and cut as many rings as possible from each slice with a canapé cutter or small biscuit cutter. You will need two rounds for each individual appetizer. Spread half of them with the *fines herbes* butter (the recipe for this is given below) and place the other slices on top. These may be garnished with a tiny border of the butter or dusted with paprika or chopped parsley. The border is made with your smallest pastry-tube nozzle.

FINES HERBES BUTTER FOR VEAL

Rub a small bowl with a clove of garlic. In it cream two tablespoonfuls of sweet butter. Add one tablespoonful of chopped parsley, one of chopped chives, a teaspoonful of chopped, fresh tarragon or chervil, if they are available, and one finely chopped anchovy fillet or one half teaspoonful of anchovy paste. Beat this to a paste with a fork and season to taste with freshly ground black pepper and salt.

The same process is employed with cold roast lamb, save that the butter differs. Slice the lamb and prepare as for the veal slices. Spread with mint butter (below) and garnish with mint leaves or freshly chopped mint.

MINT BUTTER FOR COLD ROAST LAMB

Two tablespoonfuls of creamed butter. Add one teaspoonful of chopped parsley, one tablespoonful of chopped mint that has marinated for an hour in two tablespoonfuls of wine vinegar with one teaspoonful of salt and a dessertspoonful of sugar. Drain the mint before adding to the butter and beat the mixture with a fork till thoroughly blended.

CHICKEN ROLLS

Cut cubes of cold chicken or turkey about one half inch square. Mix one-half cupful of mayonnaise with one teaspoonful of chopped, fresh tarragon or the equivalent amount of dried tarragon which has first been soaked in white wine or, failing that, fresh water. Dip the chicken into the mayonnaise and roll in paper-thin strips of prosciutto or Parma ham. If this is not available, you may try baked ham if it will roll, or cold, baked Canadian bacon from which the fat has been removed.

PORK ROLLS

Spread slices of cold roast pork or fresh ham with Escoffier Sauce Robert. Cut in strips one by four inches and roll around medium to large pickled onions. Secure with toothpicks and chill thoroughly.

TURKEY STRAWS

Cut slices of cold turkey breast or chicken breast one half inch thick. Trim well so that you have a perfect oblong of meat. Cut in strips one half inch wide and make them as uniform as possible. Dip the strips three quarters of their length into a very stiff mayonnaise which is well seasoned with lemon juice and tarragon. Roll in slivered, toasted Brazil nuts and chill thoroughly before serving. Arrange them on a tray or plate, with a small bowl of the mayonnaise and an additional bowl of the nuts in case any of your guests want an extra dunk.

Another variation of this delightful snack is to dip the turkey straws into a well-seasoned Russian dressing and then into finely grated Switzerland Swiss cheese. The important thing to remember is to leave one end undipped so that the guest does not have dressing all over his fingers.

CHICKEN ROLLS WITH TONGUE

Cut thin slices of tongue and trim them well in oblong shapes. Spread with a well-seasoned liver paste or *pâté de foie gras;* place a thin slice of chicken or turkey on this and a few chopped pistachio nuts. Roll tightly, secure with toothpick and chill.

SALAMI WITH HERBS

For the following recipes you will need the wire-mesh rack described in the introduction to this chapter, which holds these tiny cones in an upright position. You will also need a fine-grained salami; the coarser-grained has large bits of meat and fat which will break through. Have the salami sliced to paper-thinness at the delicatessen where you buy it. If they are large slices, each slice will make two cornucopias. If it is the small size salami, one to a slice. The large size, if properly sliced, will be found the more practical.

Fold the slices of salami around your finger to form a cornucopia. Pinch the edges together well and place in the rack. If they are pressed firmly and securely, they will stick together, but a brushing of white of egg will surely hold them. Chill the cornucopias in the refrigerator for half an hour then fill them from a pastry tube (one of the metal ones mentioned in the preceding chapter is best for this purpose) with the following:

For fifteen to eighteen cornucopias, one cupful of cream cheese, one tablespoonful each of chopped parsley and chives, one teaspoonful each of fresh dill and chopped chervil, and three-fourths teaspoonful of salt. If fresh herbs are not available, soak dried chervil and dill and chop them with a little chopped raw spinach for color. You will of course measure a teaspoonful of each herb after soaking, for a teaspoonful of dried ones would give a far greater yield. Blend the herbs with the cream cheese and fill the pastry tube. Let the filled cornucopias set in the refrigerator for at least an hour before serving.

These may be made in the morning and left in the refrigerator, for they never seem to spoil. I have experimented with them and found that they are quite as good the next day. These cornucopias are delicious with champagne and with almost any kind of cocktail.

SALAMI PARMIGIANA

Mix one half cupful of cream cheese, two tablespoonfuls of freshly grated Parmesan cheese, one tablespoonful of chopped chives or one tablespoonful of chopped pickled onions, and one teaspoonful of anchovy paste or one half teaspoonful of chopped and mashed anchovies. Fill the cornucopias as in the preceding recipe and chill.

If you are unable to find a good salami in your community, you may use these same recipes substituting summer sausage or bologna; or write to one of the large department stores of a big city; these usually have a complete grocery department.

BOLOGNA WITH CHEESE

Have your butcher or delicatessen salesman slice bologna for you to an almost transparent thinness on the electric slicer. Cut the slices in half and form into cornucopias. Brush the edges with egg white and allow them to set in the refrigerator for an hour. Fill with tiny balls of grated American cheese which has been mixed with French mustard and Worcestershire Sauce in the following proportions: three fourths of a cupful of coarsely grated soft cheese to one teaspoonful of Worcestershire Sauce and three fourths of a teaspoonful of French mustard. Mix well and form into tiny balls or cones that will fit into the cornucopias.

TARTAR BALLS

> 1 *pound of chopped, raw sirloin or tenderloin steak*
> ½ *cupful of chopped onions*
> 1½ *teaspoonfuls of salt*
> 1 *teaspoonful of black pepper*
> 1 *small clove of garlic, grated*
> *white of egg*
> *chopped parsley*
> *chopped toasted walnuts*

Mix the beef, onions, garlic, salt and pepper. Work well with the fingers and form into tiny balls. Dip in white of egg, chopped parsley, and nuts.

These are tantalizing, filling, and a good antidote for over-indulgence. If you notice someone getting out of control, give him half a dozen!

PARMA HAM OR PROSCIUTTO

Parma ham or prosciutto is one of the most versatile and one of the most delicious of all cold meats. It should be cut to a transparency and is delicious when served on a platter in its virgin state. Or there are many variations which may prove useful to you:

Slices of prosciutto rolled around well-spiced sweet gherkins are simple and delicious.

Rolled around a finger of cold turkey or chicken, with a little freshly ground black pepper sprinkled over it.

A slice of prosciutto rolled around a finger of Switzerland Swiss cheese is unbelievably good.

Rolled with Roquefort butter and chopped chives.

Spread a slice of Parma ham with chopped mushrooms and cream cheese and roll.

Spread slices of Parma ham with *fines herbes* butter and roll.

A slice of prosciutto rolled around a whole boneless

and skinless sardine and bountifully sprinkled with chopped parsley.

Roll slices of prosciutto around sprigs of fresh water cress so that there are tiny clumps of leaves at each end.

FORCEMEAT SANDWICH

If you have a good recipe for meat loaf which you feel is the best in the community, this may appeal to you: For a dozen sandwiches, slice twelve thin slices of the cold loaf and cut them with a small round or crescent-shaped cutter. Spread lightly with a pickle-and-olive butter made by creaming together two tablespoonfuls of butter with one teaspoonful of finely chopped olives and pickles. Press pairs of slices together and roll the edges in a mixture of paprika and freshly ground black pepper.

For the following recipes you will need tiny shells: clam shells of various types or oyster shells if they are not too well covered with growth from the sea.

SWEETBREADS IN SHELLS

Blanch and trim one pair of sweetbreads; let them soak in cold water for an hour. Drain them well and poach for about twenty minutes in boiling, salted water. Drain and place in cold water again until you are ready to mix the salad.

> *1 cupful of diced sweetbreads*
> *1 cupful of cold boiled chestnuts, diced*
> *½ cupful of finely diced cucumber*
> *mayonnaise*

Toss the ingredients together lightly and add mayonnaise to bind. Arrange in the small shells in little mounds and chill in the refrigerator. Truffle slices or finely shredded ham are good garnishings for this salad.

A salad of cold diced chicken or turkey or duck may be prepared with similar ingredients and served in the shells. This makes a delightful summer snack.

CHICKEN OR DUCK SALAD FOR SHELLS

> *1 cupful of diced chicken or duck*
> *⅓ cupful of chopped almonds*
> *1 tablespoonful of chopped parsley*
> *mayonnaise*

Mix the chicken or duck and the chopped parsley and almonds with enough heavy mayonnaise to bind. Fill the shells and decorate with capers and water cress.

* * *

If there is a really fine Chinese restaurant in your immediate neighborhood or in your community, a very easy and delicious variation for your cocktails may be bought there. Buy some of their roast pork which is one of the specialties of Chinese cooks. Have the chef slice it for you and ask him for a little of the Chinese hot mustard which outdistances the English mustard by several degrees. Arrange the pork on a plate and have a tiny dish of the mustard and one of French mustard for the more cautious guests. I advise warning signs about the hot mustard.

Chinese roast duck is another delicacy that you may buy from your restaurateur. Again, have the chef cut it for you into dainty bits, and serve it with a grinder of coarse salt at hand for seasoning.

CHEESE HORS D'OEUVRE

Cheese is probably the friendliest of foods. It endears itself to everything and never tires of showing off to great advantage. Any liquor or, I may say, any potable or any edible loves to be seen in the company of cheese. Naturally, some nationalities choose one type of companion and some another, but you very seldom find clashes of temperament in passing.

An assortment of cheese is a welcome addition to any party no matter what else is served. A huge board or tray may hold two to ten different varieties to be sliced or scooped at will, and although you have the most tempting bits of lusciousness in your repertoire, you will find there is a steady, appreciative audience at the cheese board.

Good cheese needs good companions. Fine mustard is desired by some cheese fans, so have a selection of the French and the English and the very hot Chinese varieties. Provide thin bread and butter and biscuits and crackers. The Tunbridge Wells water biscuits are to me the ultimate in cheese biscuits, but there are also really excellent American brands today.

And don't forget, some people want butter with cheese.

These are a few of the more popular types of cheese which are easy to find in all parts of the United States and which please most palates:

Canadian Cheddar, full and ripe in flavor.

New York Herkimer County Cheddars, excellent.

Famous Oregon and Wisconsin cheeses of several varieties, all good.

Switzerland Swiss and Gruyère; and be sure you get the imported, for the flavor is subtle and the texture fine.

Fine French Roquefort, the queen of all cheeses; and its cousins, Gorgonzola and Danish Bleu.

England's prize contributions: Stilton, Cheshire, and Cheddar.

The luxurious Brie and Camembert of France, which should be the consistency of thick cream. A fine American Brie that should be more appreciated than it is, is now made in Illinois and is available in many markets.

A rather close relative is the Canadian Oka made by monks in northern Canada, a truly distinguished cheese.

Taleggio from Italy and Bel Paese, one rich and full-flavored and the other delicate as an orchid.

The typically American store cheese, large and round, cut in wedges, which, if properly aged, is a delicious tidbit; and the Monterey Jack cheese which is mild in flavor.

The cream cheese brick that is a refined offspring of the Limburger family.

Danish Tilsit, which is in a class all by itself.

Liederkranz, made in America.

Goat cheese.

These are only a few of the countless varieties to be found everywhere nowadays. Whatever cheese you select, be sure it is the good *natural* product. Processed cheeses are rubbery in texture and uninteresting.

Cream cheese is a boon to hors d'oeuvre, for it is a bland and accommodating binder that takes on almost any flavor that is mixed with it. Consequently, it is one of the most convenient items in this family and one that should never be absent from your refrigerator shelves.

Cheese balls are a delightful appetizer with most drinks. Mix the ingredients and make the balls with a pair of butter paddles which have been soaking in ice water for several hours before you use them. After the balls are made and garnished, give them an hour or two to harden in the refrigerator. Serve only a few at a time, on a bed of parsley or lettuce leaves and refill the plates often, not only from popular demand, but to keep the balls cold and firm as long as possible.

CHIVE BALLS

One cupful of cream cheese, one half cupful of chopped chives, or chopped green onions if chives are not available, one teaspoonful of French mustard, one half teaspoonful of salt, two thirds teaspoonful of black pepper, freshly ground. Cream well and shape into balls.

OLIVE CHEESE BALLS

One cupful of cream cheese, one half cupful of chopped ripe olives (the tinned ones are excellent for this), one tablespoonful of butter. Cream well and form into balls the size of a marble. Roll in coarsely chopped walnuts.

CURRIED CHEESE BALLS

Chop one tablespoonful of India chutney very fine and mix well with one tablespoonful of butter and one teaspoonful of curry powder. Mix this with one cupful of cream cheese; form into balls and roll each one in freshly grated coconut.

SWISS CHEESE BALLS

One cupful of cream cheese, three tablespoonfuls of grated Switzerland Swiss cheese, two tablespoonfuls of freshly grated horse-radish, one half teaspoonful of salt. Mix these ingredients till they form a solid mass that may be rolled into balls. You may find you have to add an additional amount of cream cheese or thick cream to bind this, depending on the consistency of the grated cheese. Form into balls and roll each in coarsely ground cooked ham.

MEXICAN CHEESE BALLS

One and one half cupfuls of cream cheese, one tablespoonful each of chopped green pepper, pimiento, and onion, one half teaspoonful of salt. Mix well, form into balls and roll in pignolia nuts, or you may call them pine nuts or Indian nuts.

Roquefort cheese balls

Mix together four ounces each of Roquefort cheese and butter. Add to this one half teaspoonful of dry mustard and blend well. Form into balls the size of a marble and roll them in a mixture of finely chopped parsley and chives. I suggest a mixture of two parts chives to one part parsley.

Mushroom caps filled with Roquefort

Select twelve perfectly shaped, raw mushrooms and peel them very carefully in order to keep the smooth quality of the cap. Stuff them with the Roquefort mixture given above and sprinkle the cheese with chopped chives. The raw mushroom flavor has a peculiar sympathy of flavor with the Roquefort.

I think it delightful to have large bowls of cheese mixtures which are of a consistency that permits "dunking." Cream cheese mixed with chopped chives and sour cream, and perhaps a little green pepper and a great deal of parsley, is always welcome.

Roquefort cheese or Gorgonzola mixed with cream cheese and sour cream, with a flavoring of chopped chives and chopped raw mushrooms, is another good dunker.

Cream cheese, sour cream, and grated fresh horse-radish and a few chopped chives is another delightful addition to this family.

You may have your choice of dunkers—potato chips, pretzels, crackers, Italian bread sticks—any of them.

❧SEAFOOD HORS D'OEUVRE

A plate of cold seafood with a delicious dressing is always a very welcome addition to any cocktail party. I favor one of the sectional hors d'oeuvre trays, which will hold six or eight different types of fish and a bowl of sauce. For example:

Cold, boiled shrimps which have been poached in white wine with a bay leaf, peppercorns, and coarse salt.

Crawfish tails. Cook the cleaned crawfish in water, red wine, with allspice, bayleaf and a little tarragon and thyme.

Cubes of cold boiled lobster.

Crab legs. If you get the marvelous Dungeness crab from the Pacific coast, so much the better, for it surpasses any other crabmeat in the world.

Smoked oysters. The small ones are the most delicate.

Tiny slices of smoked salmon.

Squares of smoked sturgeon.

For a sauce I suggest a green mayonnaise, or a lobster mayonnaise *(mayonnaise rouge)*, or a Louis dressing.

GREEN MAYONNAISE

> *2 cupfuls of stiff mayonnaise*
> *1 tablespoonful of chopped chives*
> *1 tablespoonful of chopped tarragon*
> *2 tablespoonfuls of chopped parsley*
> *1 teaspoonful of chopped chervil*
> *1 teaspoonful of chopped dill*

Fold the chopped herbs into the mayonnaise and let it stand for two hours before serving.

MAYONNAISE ROUGE

Pound a lobster coral in a mortar or force it through a fine sieve and add to one cupful of mayonnaise.

LOUIS DRESSING

Two cupfuls of mayonnaise, one tablespoonful each of pickle, egg, olive, onion, green pepper, and parsley, all finely chopped. Add two tablespoonfuls of chili sauce.

A variation of this sauce is to add one half cupful of stiffly whipped cream to the dressing.

* * *

For service of this type of hors d'oeuvre you will need either small plates and forks, or toothpicks and plenty of napkins. I really prefer the former, for it is by far the kindest to your floor and to the clothes of your guests. Besides, it is far more attractive in the complete setup of your table or party. I really feel that small plates are almost a must for any gathering where hors d'oeuvre are being served. It is rather sad to see anyone, especially a man, balancing a glass in one hand and a couple of snacks in another and trying to talk and get through the room at the same time.

SALMON ROLLS

For one dozen rolls you will need twelve thin slices of smoked salmon. If it is not sliced beautifully thin and even for you at the market, I think it is safer to buy the smoked salmon in a piece and slice it yourself with a very sharp knife. Trim into oblongs about one and one half by three inches. Lay them out on a board and spread with the following mixture:

Two thirds of a cupful of cream cheese, one third teaspoonful of salt, one third teaspoonful of freshly ground black pepper, two tablespoonfuls of freshly ground horse-radish or two tablespoonfuls of horse-radish. Blend well and spread.

Roll the thin slices very carefully, as they tend to tear apart very easily. They will hold without a toothpick, but you may secure them if you wish. There should be a very attractive jelly roll effect on the ends with the contrast of the deep pink salmon and the white cheese mixture. If you want a garnish for them, mix a teaspoonful of paprika with a teaspoonful of freshly ground black pepper and dip the ends into this.

INDIVIDUAL ASPICS FOR COCKTAILS

These are among the most decorative and delightful tidbits you can serve with cocktails. A tray of them is certainly a most decorative adjunct to your buffet table; they are simple to make and may be made a day in advance and merely kept in the refrigerator till you are ready to serve them.

You will have to shop the hardware stores and restaurant equipment houses for the tiny molds that are used for pastry shells and tiny cakes. These can be found in a variety of designs and sizes from peanut-shell size to three inches in diameter. I think the small, scalloped design, the very tiny fish mold, the star, crescent, and shell are among the most attractive. These are easily available by mail from two stores in New York: Bazar Français, 666 Sixth Avenue;

and La Cuisinière, 903 Madison Avenue. Plastic egg trays or plastic ice-cube trays for round ice cubes are also excellent for these little aspics.

A basic recipe for aspic which may be used for any of the fish aspics calls for fish broth. By this I mean the broth in which a fish was cooked, always in the company of an herb bouquet tied in a small piece of cheesecloth. For most fish you will find a blend of dill, allspice (whole), tarragon, bay leaf, parsley, and chervil desirable.

ASPIC FOR FISH

Two tablespoonfuls of gelatin dissolved in one half cupful of cold water, three cupfuls of fish broth, strained and clarified with egg white. Add one teaspoonful of salt, one half teaspoonful of pepper, and one half cupful of Chablis.

After you remove the fish from the broth, strain the broth through a fine sieve, return to the pan with the white and shell of one egg, and let it simmer. Strain again through a cloth and return to the pan. Bring it to the boiling point, pour in the gelatin, and stir till it is well mixed. Allow the jelly to cool and then add the salt, pepper, and wine.

Have your aspic molds arranged on a tray with your fish in them: a tiny whole shrimp, a small bit of crabmeat, a cube of lobster, a tiny cube of salmon or halibut. Two or three capers, a tiny round of pimiento or truffle, or a thin slice of gherkin or olive on the bottom of the mold will make a more festive appearance. Fill the molds with jelly and set them in the refrigerator. Unmold. Serve with a bowl of green mayonnaise or *mayonnaise rouge.*

INDIVIDUAL MOUSSE MOLDS

Make one half the aspic recipe given above and allow to jell in the refrigerator. When cooled, beat to a froth with an egg beater or in the electric mixer. Add one and one half cupfuls of finely chopped or pounded cold fish or shellfish and one half cupful of cream, beaten stiffly. Fold together; fill tiny molds and set in the refrigerator. Unmold.

Serve these on a tray with a bowl of green mayonnaise.

Halibut, salmon, shrimp, lobster, smoked salmon, or crabmeat may be used.

FISH EN BROCHETTE

This is a most satisfactory service for a leisurely party, for it gives the guest a substantial bit of food each time he is served and allows the host to sit and enjoy his guests without jumping up every two minutes to pass the trays. It is basically a finger service, but plates will help out a great deal.

Bits of fish and garnishes strung on small metal or bamboo skewers can be arranged attractively on a large plate lined with Romaine leaves, shredded lettuce, or a bed of water cress or parsley; in the center a large, flat bowl of Russian dressing or green mayonnaise or a divided bowl which holds both. The following suggestions are but a few of the endless number of combinations possible with the aid of a riotous imagination and a satisfactory market:

Crabmeat cubes alternated with cubes of avocado which have been marinated in lemon juice to keep them green. If you are within hailing distance of the Dungeness or Seattle crabs, use the whole legs on the skewers.

Lobster cubes alternated with tiny red or yellow tomatoes, the cherry size.

Lobster cubes with cubes of marinated celery root, or knob celery, as they may call it in your neighborhood.

Small rolls of smoked salmon alternated with cubes of crisp cucumber.

Smoked salmon rolls with small cubes of baked ham and thin slices of cucumber.

Shrimp, small cherry tomatoes, and avocado cubes.

Shrimp, tiny white onions or pickled onions, and cubes of orange.

Shrimp, smoked oysters, and cucumbers.

Smoked oysters, small ones, and cubes of chicken.

Shrimp, button radishes, and anchovy fillets.

Lobster cubes, shrimp, smoked-sturgeon cubes.

Crabmeat with cucumber and bits of crisp celery.

Crabmeat and shrimp with pickled onion.

Shrimp, olive, and anchovy fillet.

JEANNE'S ANCHOVIES

For years this dish has been a great favorite with guests of Jeanne Owen. More than one person who had never liked anchovies has become a true devotee after trying them this way once.

Open a large size can of anchovey fillets, drain the oil into a bowl, and place the fillets on a plate. Mix the oil with enough chopped parsley to make a thick paste. Add a chopped shallot or two according to taste and about a tablespoonful of tarragon vinegar. Arrange the anchovies in an oblong dish and pour the sauce over them so that just a tip of each fillet shows. Serve with a fork and have plenty of Melba toast at hand for foundations. These are really a sensational dish and one everyone will like.

CAVIAR

The roe of the Russian mother sturgeon has probably been present at more important international affairs than have all the Russian dignitaries of history combined. This seemingly simple article of diet has taken its place in the world along with pearls, sables, old silver, and Cellini cups.

Just as with pearls and fine silver, many imitations of the original have come on the market. Herring and salmon mothers have given their all to imitate their Russian cousins, but there still remains but one real and satisfying caviar, the fresh Beluga, unsalted, from the Caspian Sea and the River Volga. If this is available, banish all other from your menus; use the fresh Beluga when you can get it for a special party and for special and truly appreciative guests.

As there is only one caviar, so there is only one service for it. Let us, with a great care and sentiment, bury all the caviar canapés and the caviar sandwiches, and the mixtures of caviar and smoked salmon, and place a steel and stone slab over them; inscribe on it *"Requiescat in Pace."*

Serve caviar in a glass bowl or a silver one and rest this in a bed of chopped ice, in a larger bowl. Or scoop out a hollow in a whole block of ice to hold the caviar bowl. Place on a tray and surround with tiny dishes holding: chopped hard-cooked egg, whites and yolks separate, chopped onion, quartered lemon. Thin slices of Russian black bread (to be found in most delicatessens or foreign bake shops) or pumpernickel (and the canned pumpernickel is excellent), some buttered and some not, and a few slices of Melba toast arranged on a plate complete the accessories. Your guests will dip the caviar out with a spoon or ladle and season it to their taste. You will of course need plates for this service.

Since you are splurging on this party, with caviar at a price which runs to the pinnacle of food prices, you might as well go the limit and have a choice of the two drinks most complementary to the dish—fine champagne and vodka. Serve the champagne properly cooled, and serve plenty of it. The vodka is served straight, in tiny glasses similar to a liqueur glass. If you are sure of an appreciative audience, with your caviar and champagne properly iced, your vodka of the best and your accessories perfect, you may rest assured you have given the best party of the season and one that will be appreciated for months to come.

OYSTERS

Many combinations have been suggested for oysters on the half shell, but to enjoy them at their best white wines are outstanding to complement them. They are a favorite of gourmets the world over. Your guests will appreciate such a thoughtful delicacy if you are within reach of good oysters.

Your oysters should be opened in the kitchen as needed and arranged on large trays well packed with ice. Your local caterer or hotel will be glad to rent you deep trays for this service. Or you might rent for the afternoon what is known as an ice cradle, which is filled with chopped ice with the trays placed on this. A servant can serve the guests, and offer them horse-radish, salt, pepper, lemon, or cocktail sauce as garnish. Trays of thin bread and butter, light and dark, may also be passed.

Instead of liquor, a fine Graves or Chablis, chilled, may be served, or a very dry champagne. Stout and ale are also very compatible with the oyster.

To me, this is a particularly civilized idea for entertaining and if the oysters in your section of the country are good, nothing could be more appreciated, especially at the beginning of the oyster season.

🐦EGG HORS D'OEUVRE

I enjoy toying with the idea that the so-called "old eggs" from China were the original ancestor of the hors d'oeuvre. If that is true, it was certainly a most auspicious beginning and a flattering compliment to the hen. For those mellow and flavorful bits of egg packed in clay have come down through untold ages and are as much in favor today with Chinese people (those who can still get them) as they were centuries ago.

No matter what else is served at a cocktail party, you will always find that a tray of stuffed eggs (not old!) will be one of the most popular items. These disappear more rapidly than anything else.

Cut such eggs either the long way of the egg or crosswise, and trim the bottoms so they do not roll around. The crosswise cut is by far the most decorative and will be found easier to handle. A pastry tube or metal icing set will be the most efficient method of filling the halves. This is simple and much more attractive than filling them with a spoon. (We must never forget the eye-appealing possibilities of all hors d'oeuvre.)

The following recipes are planned to make one dozen halves. Always be sure to boil one or two extra eggs, for the temperamental hen sometimes upsets your plans with a misplaced yolk or an inferior white.

DEVILED EGGS

Remove the yolks from six hard-cooked eggs and force them through a fine sieve. Add one teaspoonful of salt, one teaspoonful of dry mustard, one half teaspoonful of freshly ground, black pepper, one teaspoonful of Worcestershire sauce, one and one half tablespoonfuls of chopped parsley, and at least a tablespoonful of mayonnaise. Beat well with a fork till the mixture forms a firm paste, adding more mayonnaise if necessary. Fill the white halves, using a pastry tube, and garnish with chopped parsley or tiny strips of pimiento.

ANCHOVY EGGS

Force the yolks of eggs through a sieve and add three tablespoonfuls of chopped anchovies or two tablespoonfuls of anchovy paste, one half teaspoonful of ground pepper, one teaspoonful of salt, one tablespoonful of chopped pickled onion, and enough mayonnaise to form a stiff paste. Fill the hard-cooked white halves.

PATÉ EGGS

Mix one and one half cupfuls of liver paste or *pâté de foie gras,* one tablespoonful of creamed butter, and salt to taste. Fill the white halves of six eggs with the pâté mixture. Decorate with chopped egg white or yolk and mayonnaise mixed together to a paste and forced through a tube. These are extremely rich and should be served with plenty of green things to complement them.

SMOKED TURKEY EGGS

Fill twelve hard-cooked halves with a mixture of chopped, smoked turkey and cold wild rice mixed in equal quantities. I should advise a cup of each with the addition of one teaspoonful of salt, one half teaspoonful of black pepper, and enough mayonnaise to make a good binder, at least a quarter cupful. Fill the white halves with this, smooth them down, and decorate with tiny strips of smoked turkey.

CURRIED EGGS

Melt one tablespoonful of finely chopped onion in one tablespoonful of butter over a very low flame. Add one and one half teaspoonfuls of fine Bombay curry powder and two tablespoonfuls of thick cream and stir vigorously till this becomes a paste. Cool, and add to the yolks of six hard-cooked eggs which have been forced through a sieve. Add one teaspoonful of salt and two teaspoonfuls of finely chopped chutney and cream to a paste. Fill the egg whites with this mixture and top with grated fresh coconut.

Variations: To the curry paste you may add two thirds of a cup of either pounded cold chicken, lobster, shrimp, salmon, or crabmeat. This is added to the egg mixture, then proceed as for the plain curried eggs.

EGGS VIRGINIAN

Mash the yolks of six hard-cooked eggs and add four tablespoonfuls of finely chopped cold ham, one tablespoonful of Escoffier Sauce Robert, one tablespoonful of finely chopped gherkin, and enough mayonnaise to bind and form a paste. Fill whites of the eggs and garnish with finely chopped ham mixed with paprika.

Variation: Four tablespoonfuls of chopped tongue instead of the ham.

EGGS WITH SARDINES

Mash one cupful of boneless sardines very fine and add one teaspoonful of salt, one teaspoonful of lemon juice, and a tablespoonful of mayonnaise. Cream this with one cupful of hard-cooked egg yolk that has been passed through a sieve, and fill the whites of the eggs. Garnish with more sieved yolk mixed with chopped parsley.

Seafood eggs

Chop one and one half cupfuls of either cold crabmeat, shrimp, or lobster; add two tablespoonfuls of chopped parsley and one of chives. Mix this with one and one half tablespoonfuls of Russian dressing and fill the whites of six eggs. Garnish with chopped egg yolk or thinly sliced sweet gherkin.

Cheese eggs

Mash the yolks of six hard-cooked eggs. To this add two tablespoonfuls of creamed butter and three tablespoonfuls of grated Switzerland Swiss cheese. Blend these well and fill the whites from a pastry tube. Tiny squares or triangles of Switzerland Swiss cheese are an appropriate decoration for this one. And an extremely good egg this is, too.

Eggs tartar

This is a real "he-man" version, one that should go with much Scotch or Irish whiskey or with that delicate little number known as the French 75.

Chop, do not grind, one half pound of lean, raw steak, tenderloin preferred. Mix this with one raw egg and two teaspoonfuls of salt, one of black pepper, and two table-spoonfuls of chopped onion. Fill hard-cooked whites cut the long way with this mixture and garnish with chopped chives. Serve them very cold.

CHICKEN EGGS

Chop one cupful of cooked chicken with one half cupful of blanched and lightly toasted almonds. Add one tea-spoonful of salt and one tablespoonful of chopped tarragon. Allow this to marinate in two tablespoonfuls of white wine for two hours. Pour off any liquid and bind with mayon-naise. Fill the whites and garnish with shredded almonds.

FISH EGGS

Put hard-cooked egg yolks through the fine sieve. Add one half cupful of well-pounded tuna fish or cold salmon, one tablespoonful of chopped cucumber, one teaspoonful of salt, and bind with mayonnaise. Fill the whites with this and top with a thin slice of cucumber.

AVOCADO EGGS

Rub a bowl with garlic. In this place one half of a large (or one whole small) avocado, one teaspoonful of salt and one of black pepper, and a half teaspoonful of dry mustard.

Mash the avocado very well and add the puréed hard-cooked egg yolk gradually till you have achieved a fine textured paste for forcing through a tube. Fill the whites with this mixture and decorate with chopped egg yolk and sprigs of fresh water cress.

EGGS FINES HERBES

Chop together some parsley, chives, tarragon, chervil, and green onion till they are practically a paste. You will want about one half cupful of chopped herbs when you are through, so gauge accordingly. Sprinkle well with salt and a little cayenne. Mix with puréed hard-cooked egg yolk till the mixture forms a fine paste, adding, if necessary, a little olive oil to bind it. Fill the whites with this mixture forced through a pastry tube.

VEGETABLE HORS D'OEUVRE

I suppose even with drinking and gaiety we must still think of vitamins, but when there are such good vitamins and such pleasant, intimate friends of good cheer, who cares?

The variety of raw vegetables waiting to take a place on your hors d'oeuvre table is almost unbelievable! The array may be perfectly arranged on a huge tray of silver or glass, wood or tôle, and makes a colorful, decorative addition to your table. With this type of service, you will want two or three bowls of dressings which inspire dunking. Mayonnaise with chopped herbs, Russian dressing, and a bowl of thick sour cream with chopped chives in it can grace the center of your tray and be decorative and functional at the same time. Perhaps you have a huge pottery or glass bowl which holds plenty of cracked ice on which to arrange the vegetables. A long shallow bowl filled with finely chopped ice is ideal for green onions and radishes, which can be stuck into the ice and produce a lively effect.

One of the most charming ways to serve these raw tidbits is to have a large tray or buffet with a number of matching bowls, some holding neatly arranged mounds of vegetables, others the sauces. All the vegetables should be washed thoroughly and iced for several hours before servingtime. They may be sliced in thin slices or served in strips or, in the case of the small items, served whole, depending on the vegetable.

The following are all complementary to cocktails and pleasing to the palate: raw young turnips; young carrots; tender zucchini (or Italian squash, to some); green pepper; sweet red pepper; scallions; sliced sweet onions; cauliflower buds; broccoli buds; tiny Brussels sprouts; radishes of all descriptions; celery; Chinese cabbage; fennel, or Italian celery, as it is sometimes called; Belgian endive; tomatoes of all types, currant, cherry, tiny red and yellow pear tomatoes; large red and yellow tomatoes, sliced; raw mushrooms; raw asparagus tips; cucumber.

Let your imagination run riot in arranging them and use as many kinds as you will.

Suitable dressings: sour cream with chives; French dressing; Roquefort dressing; Russian dressing; green mayonnaise; or plain mayonnaise seasoned with curry, chutney, or mustard. The recipes for some of these are given below; others you will find in the index.

Celery, fennel, and endive may be stuffed and arranged on the trays. Suitable stuffings are listed here; you will find the recipes in the chapter on canapés: *fines herbes* butter, anchovy butter, shrimp butter, chicken spread, and ham spread; and of course all kinds of creamed cheese mixtures.

FRENCH DRESSING

> *three parts olive oil*
> *one part wine vinegar*
> *salt*
> *freshly ground black pepper*

Mix well.

ROQUEFORT DRESSING I

Add crumbled bits of Roquefort cheese to French dressing.

ROQUEFORT DRESSING II

Add crumbled bits of Roquefort cheese to a rich mayonnaise.

RUSSIAN DRESSING

> 2 cups of mayonnaise
> 1 teaspoon of dry mustard
> 2 tablespoons of finely chopped onion
> 2 ounces of caviar
> 1 tablespoon of Worcestershire Sauce

Mix together thoroughly and chill for at least one hour.

CURRY MAYONNAISE

Add two teaspoons (or to taste) of Indian curry powder to one cup of mayonnaise.

CHUTNEY MAYONNAISE

Chop chutney fine and add two tablespoons (or to taste) to one cup of mayonnaise.

MUSTARD MAYONNAISE

Add one tablespoon (or to taste) of Dijon mustard to one cup of mayonnaise.

STUFFED ARTICHOKE BUDS

These are particularly delightful snacks and are seasonable in the early spring when the tiny artichokes are available in the markets. You may have to go to the Italian markets to find the buds, for most Americans insist on the huge full-grown artichokes.

Choose the tiniest artichokes you can find; boil them for twenty-five minutes in salted water to which you have added one or two kernels of garlic, a tablespoonful of peppercorns and one half cup of vinegar. Be sure to chill them thoroughly, and then very carefully pick off the first two or three layers of leaves. With a sharp knife cut vertically through the whole artichoke to within a half inch of the bottom. If you use a nonstainless knife, be sure to keep it carefully wiped; the acid will cause a stain. Scoop out the choke in the center with a tiny vegetable scoop such as those used for melon balls. Trim the bottom so that it will stand alone and is neat and even looking. Fill with any of the following mixtures and garnish with chopped egg or parsley or with a bit of thinly sliced pickle or chopped pepper.

FILLINGS FOR ARTICHOKES

Chopped chicken and almonds mixed with mayonnaise; crabmeat flakes with Russian dressing; chopped ham with hard-boiled-egg garnish; *pâté de foie gras;* chopped shrimps with an onion mayonnaise and chopped chives.

STUFFED BEETS

Tiny young beets make a most colorful addition to the hors d'oeuvre tray and are a welcome change from other types of snack. They may be included in a vegetable arrangement. They are cooked in water to which a little vinegar is added. They must be peeled and trimmed so they will stand. Scoop out the tops and fill with chopped marinated herring and hard-boiled egg. A bit of chopped deviled ham mixed with chopped parsley is also a most complementary filling for the beets. Any of the egg fillings found in the section devoted to stuffed eggs will go well with beets, the strange, sweetish flavor of which is enhanced by various savory mixtures.

CRISP CUCUMBER RINGS

These form a delightful base for several things and are always a refreshing bit to find on a vegetable tray. For the rings choose cucumbers which have a definite slenderness—

the long, thin silhouette in other words. Score them lengthwise with a fork and wash thoroughly. The scoring gives a streak of the white flesh between the dark green strips of the skin and makes a very attractive contrast. Slice them in one half inch slices and scoop out a cup in the center of each slice. Fill with one of the following:

Shreds of smoked salmon molded into a ball. Surround with a line of finely chopped parsley so that you have the green of the skin, the white of the flesh of the cucumber, the green line of the parsley and the brilliant pink of the smoked salmon.

Finely chopped crabmeat mixed with salt, chopped chives, and mayonnaise. For one dozen cucumber rings you will need about one cupful of the crabmeat paste. Lobster meat may be treated the same way.

Cubes of cold lobster surrounded with a line of finely chopped egg and topped with *mayonnaise rouge.*

A tiny mound of cold boiled salmon with a ring of chopped parsley and topped with green mayonnaise.

A mound of chopped tuna fish and chopped sweet gherkins. A small can of tuna and two gherkins will be ample for twelve rings.

PEPPER SLICES

Green peppers have their place as appetizer bases, too. Choose the long, thin ones rather than the round, luxurious, dowager type. If you search the markets well, you will find them in varying greens. In the Italian markets, you find them in a chartreuse shade and often red-and-green-streaked ones. Cut out the stem ends, core the peppers, and remove the seeds and fibers.

Mix two cups of cream cheese with one half cup of chopped chives and two teaspoonfuls of prepared French mustard. Add one and one half teaspoonfuls of salt and four tablespoonfuls of Switzerland Swiss cheese cut into tiny cubes. When all this is well mixed and blended, fill your peppers with the mixture; press in well so that it reaches to the farthest corner and chill in the ice box for two to three hours. Just before serving, slice with a very sharp knife in slices about one quarter of an inch thick. Arrange on a plate and serve.

STUFFED TOMATOES

If you have the time, and the patience, you will find that tiny stuffed tomatoes will make one of the most decorative and delightful appetizers you can possibly serve. They may be stuffed with any chicken, tuna fish, salmon, lobster or crab mixture and garnished with chopped parsley or chopped hard-boiled eggs. They are truly one of the most refreshing bites one can eat with cocktails or highballs.

You will find an assortment of small tomatoes in the markets from June till October. The small, red cherry variety and the red pear and plum tomatoes are in for several months. The yellow ones seem to come in later, but you will find them in the early part of August and usually until October or November. I advise that when you are stuffing the tiny ones, you do not peel them unless they are quite firm. Scoop out with a small vegetable scoop and fill with your pet mixture; I favor chopped chicken or ham.

STUFFED DILL PICKLES

Small-size dill pickles—homemade ones *please*—are delicious when they are filled with a tiny bit of crabmeat mixed with Russian dressing. The seeds must be scooped out with a coffee spoon, or a larding needle, or other long sharp instrument (the tool depends on the size of the pickle). Leave only the firm outer rim of the pickle. Force the dressed crabmeat into the pickles and allow them to chill in the refrigerator for at least an hour so they will be crisp and cool to the taste. They always encourage another round of drinks.

PEGGY'S RADISHES

Spread sweet butter around the middles of young, red radishes. Wrap an anchovy fillet around each radish and secure with a toothpick. Simple, but something to remember.

✻FRUIT HORS D'OEUVRE

Along with summer comes the round of delightful, cool long drinks so conducive to lounging and lengthy conversation. A porch or terrace or garden bench, with a tray of frosty glasses and a few congenial individuals, offer a great deal to the appreciative soul.

But what of food? The rich and spicy bits that tempt us during the colder months seem revolting at this time. For summer, one classification of foods most unusual and delicious of all—fruit hors d'oeuvre. Champagne, Tom Collins, rum drinks, and most of the summer drinks complement fruits and you need not be told that there is nothing more refreshing during the hot months, or at any time in the tropics.

If you are entertaining a large number of people, here is your dish; and have reserves, for I guarantee that it will melt like summer snow. Eye-filling? Yes! Appetite-provoking? Yes! ! Thrilling to taste? Yes! ! ! It's called:

MELON MÉLANGE

Find the largest watermelon you can; chill it well; cut it lengthwise in halves. Scoop out the meat with ball cutters of various sizes. Put these balls in a separate bowl and chill them well. Smooth the inside surfaces of the melon halves and fill them with ice. Build one or two beds of ice, depending on whether you are using one half or two, on a huge tray or on a table which is waterproofed—an oval bed of ice larger, considerably larger, at the base. Fit the melon half or halves into this ice bed. A twin arrangement will look much more festive.

Resting in your refrigerator alongside the melon balls should be four cans of pineapple fingers, or two peeled fresh pineapples which have been cut into fingers and sprinkled with sugar (brown sugar is more flavorful; allow two or three tablespoonfuls per pineapple, according to size). Also, have one quart of fresh ripe strawberries which need not be hulled if they are large and firm and recently picked, one quart of ripe cherries, one quart of apricot halves, and, if you wish, one dozen ripe, firm peaches that have been peeled and quartered and covered with lemon juice and water to keep them from turning brown. Scoop out two melons, a honeydew and a cantaloupe, with the ball cutter, and squeeze the juice of two limes over the meat.

Remove the ice and water from the watermelon shells and arrange grape or strawberry leaves around the edges. Arrange your fruits in them with an eye both for effect and proper blending of flavors. When they are piled high in the shells, pour a cupful of kirsch over each half, or if they are very large melons, one and one half cupfuls. If you prefer the flavor of white wine with fruit, pour a pint of fine French Sauternes over each shell. You may prefer cognac, in which case you will need one and one half cupfuls for each shell. If you are feeling very flush after a successful day at the races or are on the verge of making a startling announcement, wait till your guests arrive and drench each shell with a good, non-vintage champagne.

In any event, you will find the mounds disappear as I warned you like snow in the summer sun. Have plates for those who want them and many toothpicks or tiny skewers so that people may spear a bit of this or that at will.

This is as gay as a strawberry festival in the Nineties and much more fun, and it is a glorious accompaniment to summer libations.

STRAWBERRIES

A famous English hostess who entertained a great deal in the summer at her large country place had a very simple idea which was always extremely popular. It was this: in addition to large trays of tempting canapés and hors d'oeuvre she always served huge bowls of strawberries, plenty of sugar, and heavy cream, arranged on tables in various parts of the garden and in the house. These were replenished after each attack by the horde; and they were always in the direct line of attack, I can assure you. Simple but satisfying.

STUFFED PINEAPPLE

The formal-looking pineapple may be scooped out with a ball cutter, after the top is sliced off and put in a safe place (it makes a decorative hat for the finished piece); fill this shell with a variety of things and plant it in a bed of ice.

Rum-soaked balls of pineapple and large ripe straw-berries are most congenial neighbors in this type of dwelling. Cherries that have been poached in a sugar syrup and plentifully drenched with cognac, and peaches treated in the same manner, mix well with the bits of fresh pineapple.

Whole or halved apricots that have been lightly poached in syrup and well steeped in cognac have a natural affinity for pineapple. With this combination a few blanched and salted almonds are delicious, or better yet, if it is summer, accompany the fruit with a dish piled high with fresh, green almonds. As you probably know, green almonds are eaten when they are well formed pods. You cut the pod open with a fruit knife, peel the tender green kernel very carefully and devour it. A lot of trouble but it is well worth the effort.

Bits of preserved ginger, pineapple, and melon balls are a particularly nice group to meet on a hot day. Soak the pineapple in a little of the ginger syrup before putting it back in the shell. Whole, fresh kumquats add a bit of gay and exotic color to this combination.

Or just a large, well-iced pineapple well filled with nothing more than strawberries and blessed with a wineglassful of kirsch will be a satisfying treat to greet any guest.

A CITRUS PLATE

I object strenuously (as before noted!) to a large glass, filled with fruit and a little whiskey and bitters poured

over it, and called an Old Fashioned cocktail. If you want
fruit with an Old Fashioned, why not serve an attractively
arranged citrus plate?

For this, slice two or three limes, depending on their
size, and two large, ripe oranges; peel a large, pink grapefruit, and wash a small basket of kumquats. In the center
of a large plate, place a bowl of powdered sugar or honey
diluted with lemon juice (juice of two lemons to a cupful
of honey). Arrange the lime slices, orange slices cut in
half, grapefruit segments and whole kumquats around it.

PICKLED AND SPICED FRUITS

If you have a stock of your own or your cook's pickles
and preserves, don't hesitate to use them with cocktails.
Pickled watermelon rind is one of the most delightful accompaniments possible, and if you have pickled crabapples
and peaches and prunes with the pungent sweet-sour syrup
that surrounds them, arrange them all on a dish and let
your friends descend on it.

The Italians have a method of preserving fruit in a very
hot mustard syrup that is one of the most unusual treat-
ments you can imagine. These are ideal for cocktail time,
served alone or with thin slices of prosciutto arranged on
a plate.

The melon is an age-old and natural ally of prosciutto
or Parma ham. The traditional method of serving a large
section of melon with slices of ham wrapped around it

presents some difficulty to the guest who has a cocktail in one hand. Besides, a roomful of people standing around plunging into great slabs of melon and trying to manage the ham is not the most attractive picture in the world. Therefore, I have streamlined this dish for the cocktail public.

HAM WITH MELON

> *1 large ripe melon; I prefer honeydew or Persian*
> *24 slices of prosciutto or Parma ham*
> *1 lemon*
> *freshly ground black pepper*

Peel and seed the melon and cut in fingers about two and one half inches long and one half inch square; you will want twenty-four fingers for this quantity of ham. Squeeze the juice of one lemon over the pieces and grind a little fresh pepper over them. Wrap each finger in a slice of prosciutto and serve within half an hour. It is wiser to make these in two or three rounds, for the melon seems to tire very quickly and is not attractive when this happens.

You may prefer to have a bowl of the melon fingers in a bowl set over cracked ice with a plate of sliced ham nearby and let your guests "roll their own." Some like chopped mint with this; use it if you care for the flavor combination.

Jeanne Owen, of the Wine and Food Society of New York, the author of *A Wine Lover's Cookbook* and one of

America's truly great cooks, has a fruit curry which is one of the most thrilling dishes anyone can eat. With her permission, I am presenting her recipe with certain adaptations for its place on the hors d'oeuvre table.

CURRY OF FRUITS

The sauce:

1½ cupfuls of rich chicken broth, or one can of consommé

2 tablespoonfuls of curry powder

1 small bottle of white wine

2 tablespoonfuls of arrowroot

⅔ of a cupful of seeded raisins puffed in warm water

2 cupfuls of finely chopped toasted Brazil nuts

2 cupfuls of freshly grated or packaged grated coconut

Heat the broth; add the curry powder and stir till dissolved or blended. Add the white wine and allow to simmer for one half to three quarters of an hour. Mix the arrowroot with a little water or broth; add it to the mixture and stir till thick. Throw in the raisins and place the sauce in a double boiler to keep warm.

The fruit:

>   20 *pineapple fingers, canned or fresh*
>   20 *melon slices or fingers*
>   5 *peaches, peeled and quartered*
>   20 *mango slices, fresh or canned*

Bananas are also delicious with this. If you can get the tiny, finger bananas, place some of them on the plate in their skins. Large bananas may be halved or quartered and left in the skins so they do not get brown.

Prepare these fruits and place them in the refrigerator to become thoroughly chilled. Serve them on a plate resting on a bed of chopped ice.

Place the plate of iced fruit on a tray with a bowl of grated fresh or desiccated coconut, a bowl of chopped or shaved almonds and a bowl of shaved, blanched Brazil nuts and, finally, a bowl of the hot curry sauce. Your guests will dip the fruit into the hot sauce and then into the nuts or coconut or both. A truly wonderful experience at any time.

You have full leeway with fruits, anything in season or something canned or preserved which appeals to you may be included in this group. But remember the fruit must be icy and the sauce must be hot.

Plates and forks for this one, too.

CHAPTER 3

CANAPÉS

HERE IS A WORLD IN ITSELF. The canapé world presents all sorts of problems and rules which have been laid down by one person and another. I think I shall disregard the majority of them and proceed under my own power and see if I can't reach a logical and fairly simple conclusion. First of all, every well-built house needs a good foundation. We have the same problem here; so let us build some foundations. Here are bread bases, toasts, biscuit and cracker bases, *brioche*, puff paste, and flaky pastry for these foundations.

CANAPÉ FOUNDATIONS

BREAD BASES

Many people cut plain bread into shapes and build their canapés on these. I feel this is an insult to the guest and represents an utter disregard for the topping. Bread dries out or becomes soggy and is usually no aid to the flavor of the canapé. The one exception, in my mind, is a heavy Russian or Swedish rye bread, or a very dark and firm pumpernickel. These are ideal bases for certain mixtures which I shall list.

Tiny French rolls and thin French bread are used for certain recipes. The rolls and "French flutes," as they are called, are, by nature, crisp and crusty and add flavor and zest to the stuffing.

Toasted bread is widely used. It may be delicately colored, freshly toasted bread or the slowly dried so-called Melba toast.

MELBA TOAST

Cut the bread in thin slices, an eighth of three sixteenths of an inch thick, and cut in various shapes for canapés. Place these on racks; the usual cake-cooling racks are ideal. Pile the racks one on top of the other with one empty rack on top. Place this stack in a 225° F. oven and leave it till the bread is thoroughly dried and of a delicate color. The toast may be stored in a tightly covered tin box for a week or more. If you are going to use rather damp pastes which might make your toast soggy, dip each toasted piece in raw white of egg and return to a warming oven or to a 150° F. oven shortly before using it. The egg white forms a resistant coating and makes the toast less absorbent.

Biscuit, or cracker, bases

Biscuits, or crackers, make ideal foundations for certain canapés but great care must be used in selecting them. I feel that some of the domestic biscuits or crackers have achieved a great deal of recent years. There are many good brands of imported cocktail biscuits to be found in the specialty shops, too.

The English biscuits, particularly the Romary, are especially prepared and baked for cocktail biscuits and are, in my opinion, a perfect base for cold or hot canapés. Most of them may be placed in tins and kept on the supply shelf.

It is plainly and simply a case of experimenting and finding the readily available biscuit that suits your own needs and adopting that one into your household scheme.

Fried toasts

Toast thinly sliced bread on one side only. Melt a generous amount of butter in a skillet, an iron one if possible, and keep the heat low. Place toasts, untoasted side down, in the butter and allow them to sauté gently till browned. Drain on paper towels.

Brioche

This deliciously light and flavorful bread of France is a most perfect companion to a great many hors d'oeuvre. It is to be found in most French bakeshops in this country in its usual headed-loaf shape. You may order it baked in a plain loaf which is more practical for canapés or in tiny molds which are called for in certain recipes.

In case you wish to make your own, here is the finest recipe I have ever found for *brioche*. You may experiment with shapes and forms till you are satisfied:

> ½ *yeast cake*
> 4 *cups flour*
> 1 *tablespoonful sugar*
> ½ *cup lukewarm water*
> 1 *teaspoonful salt*
> 1 *cup melted butter*
> 6 *eggs*

Dissolve yeast cake in lukewarm water and add one cup flour. Mix till smooth and set aside till this "sponge" doubles in size, about two hours at room temperature of 70° F.

Mix the rest of the flour, the sugar, salt, and butter till smooth, and add three eggs, not beaten. Beat this mixture for two minutes and add the rest of the eggs, one at a time, beating after each addition. Add the sponge and beat smooth. Let rise for six hours at room temperature. Beat again for three minutes and place in the refrigerator for from twelve to twenty-four hours.

To bake, remove from the refrigerator, tear off small pieces according to the size of your pans, and knead them into ball-shaped pieces. These should fill each pan two thirds to three quarters full. For the individual service you will want very small pans—about one inch in diameter. Let the dough rise again to double its bulk, brush with milk, and bake in a moderate—350° F.—oven. The length of baking time depends on the size of your pans: Forty-five minutes for a loaf; twenty-five minutes for muffin size; ten to fifteen minutes for tiny ones.

The traditional *brioche* is made in a small fluted pan and wears a topknot. It may be varied to suit your own ideas. For sandwiches, a loaf is the most practical.

Pastry is necessary in the preparation of many of the recipes in this book. I include two of my recipes which are particularly adapted to the service of all sorts of hors d'oeuvre—canapés, *barquettes, bouchées, allumettes,* and turnovers.

PUFF PASTE

> 1 pound flour
> 1 teaspoonful salt
> 1 pound butter
> 1 cup ice water

Mix the flour and the salt and form a circle with them on a pastry board. Pour some of the ice water into the center and work it into the flour with your fingers, adding additional ice water as needed for a stiff paste. Place this paste in the refrigerator for thirty minutes.

Roll the paste on a floured board one quarter inch thick, taking care to keep it longer than it is wide. Spread the surface with the butter and fold in the edges to make an even rectangle. Fold the rectangle over twice, napkin fashion, so that you have three thicknesses of paste. Roll into a long narrow strip one quarter inch thick. Fold again, as before, and turn it one quarter of the way around. Roll again and repeat the process till you have rolled it four times in all, turning the dough one fourth of the way each time. After the fourth and final turn, fold the paste from each end to the center, then double, making four thicknesses. Wrap in waxed paper and place in the refrigerator till ready to bake.

Puff paste should be baked on the following schedule: 500° F. for the first five minutes. Then reduce the temperature 50° F. each five minutes till the paste is browned. If you are baking shells, or *bouchées,* do not brown them too much if they have to be placed under the broiler later, for they are liable to burn on second cooking.

To cut *bouchées:* Roll the paste one quarter inch thick and cut with a fluted cutter the size and shape you want. Cut small rounds from the center of half the pieces and attach these—the rims—to the whole rounds; brush both pieces with a little water first and gently press the edges together. The tiny centers may be used for canapé bases or for cheese puffs if you sprinkle them with a little grated Parmesan and Swiss cheese.

Cut oblong or round pieces for turnovers.

FLAKY PASTRY

> 2½ cups of flour, sifted
> 1 teaspoon of salt
> 12 tablespoons of butter, cut in pieces
> 3–4 tablespoons of ice water

Put the flour in a heap on a pastry board or in a large bowl and make a hollow in the top of the heap. Into this put the butter and salt. Blend the flour and butter with your finger tips until it is fairly well mixed and has a mealy consistency. Do not knead it roughly; just flake it gently. Add a little ice water—just enough to work the dough into a ball; do not add too much water. Roll the ball of dough in waxed paper and chill for half an hour.

This paste can be used for *barquettes,* tarts, and most turnovers.

For *barquettes,* roll very thin and line tiny boat-shaped *barquette* or tart pans. Fill the centers with rice to prevent burning or breaking during baking. If the tarts are to be reheated later, do not finish browning them. Bake in a

425° F. oven until done to the necessary state of brownness. Discard the rice.

Both the above pastes will keep several days in the refrigerator before cooking.

✺ BUTTERS

The following basic butters are listed here as a reference so that the recipes need not be repeated throughout the book. Not only are these useful for canapés and sandwiches, but they fill a need very often for cold snacks and sauces.

FINES HERBES BUTTER

Chop together two cupfuls of parsley picked from the stems, a handful each of fresh spinach leaves and water cress, chives to taste, and any of the following fresh herbs which are available, a few leaves of each to make a blend of flavors: fresh chervil, tarragon, basil, dill, thyme, or sorrel. Dried herbs may be soaked in a little white wine for two hours and then chopped. When chopped to a paste, add one teaspoonful of salt and either one teaspoonful of anchovy paste or two finely chopped anchovy fillets. Cream this with one half pound of butter till the herbs have been thoroughly blended and the butter is completely green.

ANCHOVY BUTTER NO. 1

Pound twelve anchovy fillets in a mortar or chop them till they are creamy. Blend with one quarter of a pound of butter and a few drops of lemon juice, and force through a fine sieve.

ANCHOVY BUTTER NO. 2

Pound or chop very fine twelve anchovy fillets and the yolks of two hard-boiled eggs. Blend with one quarter of a pound of butter and force through a sieve.

ROQUEFORT BUTTER

Blend together to a smooth paste one quarter of a pound each of Roquefort cheese and sweet butter.

CHUTNEY BUTTER

Cream one quarter of a pound of butter and add two tablespoonfuls of finely chopped chutney. This is improved by the addition of a little curry powder; the amount has to be left to your own taste.

Lobster butter no. 1

Add one mashed lobster coral to one quarter of a pound of butter. Season with one half teaspoonful of salt and a little fresh dill if available. Force through a fine sieve.

Lobster butter no. 2

One quarter of a pound of butter creamed with the same amount of finely chopped cooked lobster and one half teaspoonful of salt, one half teaspoonful of freshly ground pepper, and a few grains of paprika. This is much better if forced through a sieve.

Shrimp butter

Cream one quarter of a pound of butter with a cupful of finely chopped cooked shrimp, one half teaspoonful of salt, a few drops of lemon juice, and a few grains of freshly ground pepper. Force this through a fine sieve or not, as your taste decides.

Smoked salmon butter

Cream one quarter of a pound of butter with the same quantity of chopped or pounded smoked salmon and one half teaspoonful of freshly ground black pepper. Force through a fine sieve.

STURGEON BUTTER

Cream one quarter of a pound of butter with one cupful of finely chopped smoked sturgeon. A few grains of pepper and one half teaspoonful of salt are added to this.

GARLIC BUTTER

Crush several cloves of garlic and cream with one quarter of a pound of butter and one half teaspoonful of salt. This is a matter of "stop and go," for you know better than I your capacity for garlic flavor. So, let your own taste guide you.

PEPPER BUTTER

One half cupful of finely chopped green pepper and one half cupful of chopped pimiento, both of which are well drained, are creamed with one quarter of a pound of butter and one half teaspoonful of salt and passed through a fine sieve.

SARDINE BUTTER

Mix one cupful of finely mashed, boneless and skinless sardines with an equal quantity of butter and the juice of one half or one whole lemon. Force through a fine sieve.

MUSHROOM BUTTER

Cream one cupful of finely chopped, raw mushrooms
with one quarter of a pound of butter, one half teaspoonful
of salt, and a few grains of freshly ground black pepper.
Force through a fine sieve.

TOMATO BUTTER

Peel and seed one or two firm tomatoes. Chop the flesh
very fine; season well with salt and freshly ground black
pepper and drain. Cream the pulp with one quarter of a
pound of butter that has a few drops of onion juice blended
with it. The amount of butter will vary with the quality
and firmness of the tomatoes; you may need more than
one quarter of a pound. Force through a fine sieve.

HORSE-RADISH BUTTER

Cream together one quarter of a pound of butter with
two ounces of grated fresh horse-radish and one ounce of
grated Switzerland Swiss cheese. Force through a fine sieve.

CURRY BUTTER

Sauté two finely chopped shallots in a tablespoonful of
butter. Add one to two tablespoonfuls of curry powder,
one teaspoonful of arrowroot, and two tablespoonfuls of

heavy cream; stir till this is a thick paste and let it cool. Cream with one quarter of a pound of butter and force through a fine sieve.

PIQUANT BUTTER

Chop together one tablespoonful of capers, one of chives, two small sweet gherkins, one anchovy fillet, three or four pickled onions, and a few leaves of fresh tarragon. When they are finely chopped, cream with one quarter of a pound of butter and force through a fine sieve.

MUSTARD BUTTER

Blend one or two teaspoons of dry mustard (or to taste) into one quarter of a pound of butter.

SPREADS

ROQUEFORT SPREAD

Force one half pound of Roquefort cheese through a fine sieve with one quarter pound each of butter and cream cheese. Cream the mixture, adding one half teaspoonful of dry mustard and two tablespoonfuls of cognac. This may be stored in a glass jar or stone crock and kept for a couple of weeks.

Variation: Add a tablespoonful of chopped chives to the spread, or two tablespoonfuls of chopped raw mushrooms, after the mixture is creamed. In this case, use it at once.

STILTON SPREAD

Force one half pound of good Stilton cheese through a sieve with one quarter pound each of butter and cream cheese. Add two tablespoonfuls of port wine and blend. Store in a crock or jar.

ANCHOVY SPREAD NO. 1

Chop twelve anchovy fillets very fine and add to one half pound of cream cheese and three tablespoonfuls of chopped pickled onion. Blend well.

ANCHOVY SPREAD NO. 2

Twelve chopped anchovy fillets, one tablespoonful of chopped dill, and two tablespoonfuls of chopped chives are creamed with one cupful of cream cheese.

CHUTNEY SPREAD

Three tablespoonfuls of chutney, two tablespoonfuls of chopped preserved ginger, two tablespoonfuls of grated fresh coconut and two teaspoonfuls of curry paste are creamed with one half pound of cream cheese. Two table-spoonfuls of chopped blanched almonds may be added to this instead of the coconut.

TONGUE SPREAD

Chop a half pound of cold smoked tongue very fine. Add one tablespoonful each of chopped gherkin and chopped chives or shallot, one chopped hard-boiled egg, and one teaspoonful of French mustard. Bind this with sufficient mayonnaise to make a stiff paste.

CUCUMBER SPREAD

Wash a cucumber well and cut it in half the long way. Scoop out seeds and center pulp. Shred the remainder on a coarse shredder, drain, and mix with two tablespoonfuls of chopped chives or two tablespoonfuls of grated onion. Cream with one half pound of cream cheese and one teaspoonful of salt. If the cucumbers are on the watery side, you may need more cream cheese to make the spread the proper consistency.

CHIPPED BEEF SPREAD

Chop one cup of freshly sliced dried beef. Mix with one and one half teaspoonfuls of dry mustard, two tablespoonfuls of sherry, and one cup of cream cheese.

HAM SPREAD NO. 1

Chop one half pound of cold baked ham with three sweet gherkins and one teaspoonful of dry mustard. Moisten with a little mayonnaise.

HAM SPREAD NO. 2

Chop one half pound of cold baked ham or pound it in a mortar. Add one to two tablespoonfuls of chopped chives according to taste, and one half cup of chopped ripe olives —the canned chopped olives from California are excellent for this purpose. Moisten this with a little mayonnaise and blend well till it is a smooth paste.

HAM SPREAD NO. 3

To one half pound of cold baked ham, finely chopped, add one half cup of shredded Switzerland Swiss cheese, three chopped gherkins, and a tablespoonful of French mustard, and moisten with a little mayonnaise.

Variation: Add two tablespoonfuls of chopped egg yolk to this mixture.

HAM SPREAD NO. 4

To one half pound of chopped ham add one half cup of chopped olives and one half cup of chopped Brazil nuts. Moisten with mayonnaise.

HAM SPREAD NO. 5

Chop one half pound of cold baked ham. Chop six or eight mushrooms which have been sautéed in a little butter. Combine and add one half teaspoonful of salt and one teaspoonful of freshly ground black pepper, and moisten with a little mayonnaise.

HAM SPREAD NO. 6

One cup of chopped cold ham, one cup of chopped cold rare beef, one and one half teaspoonfuls of dry mustard, and enough mayonnaise to moisten.

HAM AND CHICKEN SPREAD

One cup of finely chopped cooked ham, one cup of finely chopped cooked chicken, one half cup of chopped chives, one half cup of chopped Brazil nuts, three chopped gherkins and enough mayonnaise to moisten.

HAM AND TONGUE SPREAD

One cup of chopped cooked ham, one cup of chopped cooked tongue, two teaspoonfuls of Escoffier Sauce Robert, and enough mayonnaise to moisten.

MUSHROOM SPREAD

Mix one teaspoonful of onion juice with one quarter pound of cream cheese. Add one half cup of chopped raw mushrooms and salt to taste.

SWISS CHEESE AND OLIVE SPREAD

Two cups of grated Switzerland Swiss cheese, three tablespoonfuls of chopped olives, two tablespoonfuls of chopped green pepper are thoroughly mixed. Moisten this with enough mayonnaise to make a thick paste.

SWISS CHEESE AND EGG SPREAD

Sieve the yolks of six hard-cooked eggs and blend them with two cups of finely grated Switzerland Swiss cheese and salt to taste. Add enough mayonnaise to moisten.

CHEESE AND ANCHOVY PASTE

One and one half cups of grated Gruyère cheese, two tablespoonfuls of Escoffier Sauce Robert or two tablespoonfuls of tomato catsup, two chopped anchovy fillets, and two chopped hard-cooked eggs. Blend these well and moisten with a little mayonnaise if necessary.

CHICKEN AND CHEESE SPREAD

One and one half cups of finely chopped cold chicken, one and one half cups of grated Switzerland Swiss cheese, mayonnaise to moisten, and one half cup of chopped blanched almonds.

SHRIMP SPREAD

Chop two cups of cold cooked shrimp, or tinned ones, with a handful of parsley leaves and two sweet gherkins. Add mayonnaise to bind and salt to taste.

CRABMEAT SPREAD

Chop two cups of crabmeat with one half cup of diced celery, one hard-cooked egg, and a handful of parsley leaves. Bind this with mayonnaise and salt to taste.

LOBSTER SPREAD

Two cups of lobster meat, one hard-cooked egg, one large tomato which has been peeled and from which all seeds have been removed. Chop these together very fine and add one teaspoonful of salt and some paprika. Bind with mayonnaise.

TUNA FISH SPREAD NO. 1

Mash thoroughly one seven-ounce can of tuna fish. Add two tablespoonfuls of chutney, chopping the large pieces well, one tablespoonful of chopped chives, and one tablespoonful of chopped egg yolk. Add enough mayonnaise to moisten and a little lemon juice if desired.

TUNA FISH SPREAD NO. 2

One seven-ounce can of tuna fish thoroughly mashed. Add one cup of chopped olives, a teaspoonful of grated onion, and a few drops of lemon juice. Blend and add enough mayonnaise to moisten.

BEEF SPREAD

One half pound of rare roast beef chopped with five or six pickled walnuts, one teaspoonful of dry mustard, and a tablespoonful of freshly grated horse-radish. Moisten with enough mayonnaise to bind.

VEAL SPREAD

Rub a chopping bowl with garlic. In it chop one half pound of cold veal and three or four anchovy fillets very fine. Add two teaspoonfuls of Escoffier Sauce Diable and enough mayonnaise to bind.

CHICKEN SPREAD NO. 1

Chop two cups of cooked chicken or turkey (the dark meat is far more flavorful for this). Add one half cup of chopped ripe olives, salt to taste, freshly ground pepper, and a little mayonnaise to bind. The more finely chopped the chicken, the more delicate and attractive the spread.

CHICKEN SPREAD NO. 2

Two cups of cold chicken, a few leaves of fresh tarragon, a few leaves of parsley, a few chives, and three small sweet gherkins chopped together to a paste. Bind with a little mayonnaise. Salt to taste.

CHICKEN SPREAD NO. 3

Two cups of cooked chicken, dark meat if possible, one half cup of blanched almonds chopped very fine. Add two tablespoonfuls of grated pineapple, which has been drained very well, or one and one half slices of pineapple chopped very fine. If this is not enough liquid to bind, resort to a little mayonnaise.

CHICKEN SPREAD NO. 4

One cup each of cold chicken and cold stuffing, well flavored and spiced, one half cup of Brazil nuts, a few leaves of parsley, a few tarragon leaves, and one half teaspoonful of salt. Chop very fine and blend to a smooth paste.

CHICKEN SPREAD NO. 5

One and one half cups of cooked chicken, one half cup of pignolia nuts (pine nuts or Indian nuts to you, or you, or you, depending on where you live), two pimientos, a few leaves of parsley, one shallot. Chop the chicken and pimiento; add the finely chopped shallot and parsley and the whole pignolia nuts. Bind with chili sauce to make a firm paste. Salt to taste and add a few grains of cayenne.

CURRIED CHICKEN PASTE

Chop shallots or small white onions very fine, enough to make two tablespoonfuls. Melt this in a pan with one tablespoonful of butter. Add two thirds of a cup of white wine and one tablespoonful of curry powder, and thicken with a scant tablespoon of arrowroot. When this is cooled, add to it one cup of finely chopped chicken, one half cup of finely chopped almonds, two tablespoonfuls of chutney, and a few grains of salt. Use grated fresh coconut for a garnish with this one.

CHICKEN MARRON SPREAD

Purée four or five cooked chestnuts. Mix these with one cup of chopped chicken meat, two tablespoonfuls of finely chopped celery, salt and pepper to taste, and enough mayonnaise to bind.

RILLETTES DE TOURS— (*an excellent spread*)

Immortal Rabelais writes of this original recipe for *rillettes*, which are made with odds and ends of pork and used as a pâté or just spread on a piece of crisp French bread. They are served as an hors d'oeuvre in France or in America where French restaurants are run by Frenchmen.

Choose fine leaf lard at the pork butcher's and ask him to put it through the meat grinder. Four or five pounds will do. Put the ground leaf lard in a large pan on a slow fire and allow it to fry out. Strain the melted lard but keep the residue. Put the melted lard on the flame once more, and add four ounces of water; this will keep the meat from frying. Put the pork meat, about four pounds, odds and ends with bones, etc., in the lard, and allow to simmer four or five hours. Drain from the fat and free the meat from the bones. Mince the meat, season it to taste, put in the saucepan once more, with the original residue from the lard. Add a very little melted lard, just enough to thoroughly blend. Put up in jars or glasses, being careful to break all bubbles or "air pockets." The lard will come to the top and protect the meat.

The rest of the lard can be used in the kitchen. It is almost as fine as butter for cooking, being perfectly pure.

HAZELNUT SPREAD

Grind one half pound of toasted salted hazelnuts very fine. Blend these with enough butter to form a thick paste. This is delicious by itself or blended with ham or tongue for a canapé.

CANAPÉS

SHRIMP CANAPÉS

Spread rounds of toast with shrimp butter. Arrange two small, or one large, shrimp on top and decorate with a bit of thick mayonnaise, a little chopped egg, and chopped chives.

ANCHOVY TOMATO CANAPÉS

Spread round water biscuits, or rounds of crisp toast, with anchovy paste or anchovy butter. Place a half-inch slice of peeled tomato on each biscuit and arrange anchovy fillets in bar formation on the tomato. Alternate with rows of chopped hard-cooked egg.

ANCHOVY VEAL TOASTS

Spread rounds of toast with anchovy butter and cover each toast with a thin slice of cold roast veal. Top the veal with finely chopped tuna fish mixed with enough mayonnaise to hold it together. Decorate with chopped parsley. This is a variation of the *vitello tonnato* of the Italians, and a delicious combination it is.

SARDINE CANAPÉS

Spread oblong pieces of toast or water biscuits with garlic butter. Take one skinless and boneless sardine for each canapé, slip onion rings over each sardine and place on the toasts. Use finely chopped egg and chives for decoration.

SARDINE AND EGG CANAPÉS

Spread oblong toasts or biscuits with garlic butter and arrange egg slices in the middle of each toast. Arrange a sardine on each bed of sliced egg and cover with green mayonnaise.

ROQUEFORT CANAPÉS

Spread rounds of toast or biscuits with Roquefort butter and sprinkle generously with chopped walnuts. Delightful with wines or vermouth apéritifs.

CHICKEN AND ALMOND CANAPÉS

Spread oblong toasts or thin oblong water biscuits with sweet butter. Alternate thin strips of cold chicken or turkey with rows of chopped blanched almonds and decorate with thin strips of green pepper.

BRAZILIAN CANAPÉS

Spread oblong toasts very thickly with *foie gras* or a good liver paste. Garnish with slices of toasted Brazil nuts in a pleasant pattern. (See chapter on accessories for Brazil nut recipe.)

HARLEQUIN CANAPÉS

Butter rectangular toasts with *fines herbes* butter. Cover with a thin row of finely chopped tongue, a row of chopped egg yolk, a row of chopped white meat of chicken, a row of chopped ham, and a row of chopped egg white. Decorate the edges with a tiny line of chopped parsley.

DANISH CANAPÉS

Spread rectangular canapés with smoked salmon butter. Alternate tiny strips of smoked salmon with strips of marinated herring. Decorate with a thin line of red caviar in the middle and a line of chopped chives around the edges.

LOBSTER CANAPÉS

Spread rectangular toasts with lobster butter and arrange thin slices of lobster meat along the middle; flank on one side with chopped egg white and on the other with chopped egg yolk.

CHINESE CANAPÉS

Spread rounds of toast with Roquefort butter. In the center of each toast, place a well-drained preserved lichee nut and top with a tiny dot of pimiento.

RED CAVIAR CANAPÉS

Mix one teaspoonful of onion juice and the juice of half of one lemon with one cupful of cream cheese. Form a crown of this mixture on rounds of toast with a pastry tube. Fill the center with a few grains of red caviar and decorate the edge with chopped chives.

CHEESE AND HAM CANAPÉS

Cover rounds of toast with any of the ham spreads. Cover with a round of Switzerland Swiss cheese and decorate with a slice of hard-boiled egg and chopped chervil, parsley, and chives.

CANAPÉS ARGENTEUIL

Spread rectangular pieces of bread with a mixture of butter and grated Switzerland Swiss cheese (equal proportions, in amounts according to the number of canapés). On half of these canapés place two small asparagus tips which have been marinated in French dressing and thoroughly drained and on the others, a quarter of a small tomato. Decorate with tiny strips of Switzerland Swiss cheese and a little chopped egg yolk.

GRUYÈRE CANAPÉS

Cream one third of a pound of butter with one third of a pound of grated Gruyère cheese. Add two teaspoonfuls of Escoffier Sauce Robert and salt and pepper to taste. Spread on rounds of toast with a pastry tube and decorate with radish slices and water cress.

GRUYÈRE AND HAM CANAPÉS

Mix one cup of shredded Gruyère cheese with two tablespoonfuls of butter and season with English mustard to taste. Spread on rounds of toast; cover with coarsely chopped cold ham and decorate with chopped parsley.

SALAMI CANAPÉS

Spread rounds of toast with *fines herbes* butter. Place a thin slice of salami on each round and a slice of hard-boiled egg on top. Use thinly sliced pimiento for decoration.

CANAPÉS WITH BRIOCHE

Some famous French hostess supposedly started the fashion for the recipe below and created a sensation in her salon. I am sure a reputation and a leading position in any town can be built up if you serve enough of them for they are as contagious as measles. One good friend of mine can eat a dozen of them at one sitting.

It is my favorite canapé, and is one of the simplest in the world. It is called:

BRIOCHE EN SURPRISE

Slice *brioche* in slices one quarter of an inch thick and cut in rounds with a canapé cutter or a small biscuit cutter. Spread the rounds with mayonnaise. On half the slices place a very thin slice of raw onion, just the size of the round, and salt it well. Place another slice of *brioche* on top; roll the edges first in mayonnaise and then in finely chopped parsley.

Not only is this delicious, but it is one of the most decorative canapés you can make, for the edging of brilliant green enchances the golden yellow of the *brioche* and makes it a most appetizing tidbit.

This same process may be used for tiny anchovy canapés. Spread the rounds of *brioche* with *fines herbes* butter and place fillets of anchovies on one half of the slices. Top with a second slice of the buttered *brioche;* roll the edges in mayonnaise and then in chopped parsley.

If you have the patience to make the tiniest of *brioches* following the recipe I gave at the beginning of this chapter, you will have an admirable foundation for a great many canapés and hors d'oeuvre. This bread's delicate texture and flavor make it something apart for appetizers. It complements any spread or butter and is ideal for a blend of highly refined flavors.

These tiny *brioches* are unbelievably good when stuffed with *foie gras.* You may cut a tiny round at the bottom and scoop out a bit of the bread, stuff the cavity, and place the round back in place securing it with a dot of butter. Or you may split *brioches* and fill the centers with *foie gras.*

Ham and chicken, too, are flavors that are delightful with *brioches.*

I mentioned before that almost any of the spreads may be used; I have stressed the *foie gras* because the two flavors are so very companionable.

STUFFED BREAD RINGS

For this process you need patience and determination, so don't try to perform it at the last minute and expect marvels.

You will need the very thin loaves known in the French bakeshops as French *flutes,* or thin French rolls if the former are not available, though almost any bakeshop that makes good crusty French bread will make the *flutes* for you on order. Cut the loaf or rolls in half crosswise and scoop out the center so that only the crisp tubes of crust and a little of the white center for contrast in texture are left. Fill with any of the mixtures given below and allow to set, but not so long that the crust gets soggy. Slice with a very sharp knife in slices three eighths to one half inch thick, and arrange on a platter.

CREAM CHEESE AND PISTACHIO FILLING

Cream one and one half cupfuls of cream cheese with three tablespoonfuls of chopped chives and a tablespoonful of chopped parsley. Add one teaspoonful of French mustard, one half teaspoonful of salt, and one half cup of pistachio nuts. Force the mixture into the loaves. Allow to set for half an hour before slicing. Be sure that you pack the cheese in tightly so as to get even slices. This same mixture may be used substituting long thin strips of Swiss cheese for the pistachio nuts; they must be inserted lengthwise in the tubes of crust.

TARTARE FILLING

Here is a hearty, masculine version of stuffed bread which has never failed to be satisfying and to cause pleasant comments; I like it for its rib-sticking satisfaction after strenuous exercise or long walks in the country:

After you have removed the center from the loaf, spread the cavity well with garlic butter, and see that it is good and strong with garlic flavor. Force into the shell raw, chopped steak, not hamburger but the best lean steak specially chopped by the butcher for you. Let this set for a short time and slice in one-half-inch slices. You will want plenty of salt and freshly ground pepper with this, and let guests salt for themselves. Have a dish of green onions handy, too; they are one of the best friends of raw beef.

Any of the ham or chicken spreads make admirable fillings for these rings of bread. A few whole almonds with the chicken fillings is a very smart idea, and with the ham spreads a few toasted Brazil nuts in the center of the loaf add a bit of variation.

CURRIED CHICKEN FILLING

> 1½ *cupfuls of finely chopped chicken*
> ½ *cupful of chopped blanched almonds*
> 1 *teaspoonful of chutney sauce*
> 2 *tablespoonfuls of grated fresh coconut*
> ¾ *cupful of curry sauce*

The sauce:

Melt one tablespoonful of butter in a skillet. Add one tablespoonful of curry powder and blend well. Add two tablespoonfuls of white wine and one half cupful of cream mixed with two egg yolks. Stir briskly till the mixture thickens. Remove from the fire and allow to cool.

When the sauce is cooled, mix it with the chicken, nuts, chutney, and coconut, and force the paste into the hollowed bread. Let this set for one and one half to two hours before serving.

❧TINY CHOUX

To add variety to your canapé tray, try tiny *choux* as a base or shell for spreads. They are simple to make, attractive to the eye, and delicious to the taste.

Here is a recipe perfected by the Switzerland Cheese Association, Inc., and one that is particularly suited to hors d'oeuvre:

> *1 pint of milk*
> *1 cupful of flour*
> *2 ounces of grated Switzerland Swiss cheese*
> *½ teaspoonful of salt*
> *¼ pound of butter*
> *5 eggs*
> *¼ teaspoonful of nutmeg*

Heat the milk and butter over a flame until the butter melts; add the sifted flour, all at once, and stir briskly till it forms a ball in the center of the saucepan. Add the unbeaten egg yolks and the grated cheese and beat well. Fold in the stiffly beaten whites. With the aid of a pastry tube, drop in tiny balls on a buttered pan, and bake in a moderate oven (375° F.) for about forty minutes, or until they are a deep yellow and free from moisture.

You will find that almost any of the spreads will be effective in these cases; and if the day or room is hot, they are ideal, for canapés have a tendency to melt and become very tired looking on a plate. *Choux,* however, keep their freshness and starchy appearance long after their sisters and cousins, the toasts and biscuits.

Fill these shells with pâté of your own making or any of the prepared pâtés. Top them with a little chopped egg or parsley.

Or make an avocado purée by forcing an avocado through a fine sieve into a bowl which has previously been well rubbed with garlic. Add salt and pepper to taste and one heaping teaspoonful of toasted bread crumbs. Mix these together well and fill the *choux.*

The following are several rather unusual mixtures that are excellent fillings for *chou* cases:

SALPICON DE CONCOMBRE

Chop a large cucumber very fine and salt and pepper it well. Let the chopped pulp drain through a cheesecloth till the liquid is well removed. Bind with a heavy mayonnaise and fill the shells. A bit of grated onion and chopped parsley are welcome additions, too.

Asparagus purée

Force fifteen or twenty freshly cooked asparagus tips through a fine sieve. Salt and pepper well, add a teaspoonful of chopped chives, one of chopped parsley, and bind with a heavy mayonnaise. Fill the shells with this mixture and chill.

Salpicon of celery root

Poach two medium-sized celery knobs in white wine till tender. Peel and dice into small cubes. Mix with salt, pepper, chopped chives, and capers. Bind with a stiff mayonnaise and chill.

Salpicon à la reine

Chop one cupful of white meat of chicken, one half cupful of chopped cooked mushrooms, and one quarter cupful of blanched almonds rather coarsely. Salt and pepper to taste, add a few grains of nutmeg, and bind with mayonnaise.

RAW BEEF PASTE

Raw meat recipes cause great controversy, but the men always enjoy it; and when the women overcome their initial squeamishness, they become fans, too. Nothing is more delicious when properly seasoned and very tender.

> *1½ cupfuls of finely chopped, lean, raw beefsteak*
> *½ cupful of chopped, raw onions*
> *1 raw egg*
> *1 teaspoonful each of: capers, chopped chives, chopped parsley, salt, freshly ground pepper, and Escoffier Sauce Diable*

Make a crown of the raw beef in a bowl and drop the egg and the seasonings in the center. Blend it well with your hands until it is a smooth paste. Chill thoroughly and fill the shells just before serving.

There are endless combinations that may be used for this type of service. I have tried to give you a few basic ideas and will trust your inventiveness to go the rest of the way. Cold meats and fish mixed with aspic jelly, fish and meat salads, and all the various spreads are additional ideas. You will find the *chou* a most decorative and satisfactory service.

CHAPTER 4

COCKTAIL SANDWICHES

AMERICA is a confirmed sandwich nation. Everywhere you go you find sandwich stands, sandwich shops, and nine out of ten people seem to stick to the sandwich-and-glass-of-milk or cup-of-coffee luncheon. America has developed variety in fillings, breads, and shapes, from the four-decker combination to the pale slab of white bread with a paper-thin slice of meat and much floury gravy poured over all to a vast array of really good sandwiches that distinguish our menus.

It is no wonder, then, that the cocktail sandwich has come more and more into vogue. Men like this sandwich, for it has a substantial quality that is found in no other type of hors d'oeuvre and women seem to forget the calorie content of bread persists in the cocktail sandwich.

First cousin to that aristocratic and refined member of the family, the English tea sandwich, the cocktail version should be commanding in appearance and richly attired in a simple way. The bread should be thin enough to be almost revealing, well filled, the sandwich large enough for only two bites and tailored to the last degree of perfection. Stars, crescents, tigers, rabbits, and four-leaf-clover shapes may be acceptable for tea; but for cocktails—ah, ah! Thin rectangular fingers or small squares, diamonds, and rounds should be the only shapes ever seen on a tray served with drinks.

Try to find the most interesting breads in your community and always use them for such sandwiches. In almost any town or city today, there is some semblance of variety offered by commercial bakeries; and there are many recipes for interesting breads to be made at home for this service. I think the dark, heavier-textured breads are most desirable for the cocktail tray. There are many different types of pumpernickel and rye breads which are excellent. The Scandinavians, all of whom are sandwich lovers, have developed a dozen different types of dark, meaty breads; the Danish pumpernickel, dark and light; the Swedish rye breads; the coarse, very dark bread of the Russians. All these are remarkably good with drinks. There seems to be a renaissance these days in this country for the very close grained homemade type of bread which we all knew as children. One energetic woman in the East perfected a firm white bread which sold over the entire seaboard, with the result that many commercial bakeries are now offering a loaf of this same type. The vogue is growing in every section of the country. Then, there is the delicious egg bread that is so much a part of the Jewish food tradition, and its cousin, the *brioche*. The recipe I gave for this in the preceding chapter may be used, baked in a loaf pan; it makes perfect sandwiches.

Have bread cut very, very thin for cocktail sandwiches. If you have a very sharp knife and a good eye, you may be able to cut it at home; otherwise, ask your delicatessen manager to put it on his electric slicer and cut it as thin as possible. Have him cut it the long way of the loaf, for that way you save labor and get more sandwiches per loaf. If bread is very soft and new, it should be placed in the refrigerator for an hour or two before slicing.

Have fresh butter in a bowl and let it get very soft and creamy. It will harden later in the refrigerator when the sandwiches are made.

Have spreads ready and soft, meat sliced, knives sharp, and off you go. Pile the sandwiches on a tray as they are cut; cover them with waxed paper and a damp cloth, and give them at least an hour or two in the refrigerator before serving.

Cut sandwiches in fingers, about one by three or two inches, or cut with a round cutter.

Most of the canapé spreads may be used for sandwiches and some of the butters listed in that chapter will enhance the flavor of meats in sandwiches; use them occasionally instead of the usual sweet butter.

✥FILLINGS

Here are some of the "regulars":

White meat of chicken or turkey on white bread, preferably.

White meat of chicken or turkey with chutney butter or curry butter.

Chopped chicken with chopped almonds or Brazil nuts.

Chopped chicken with sweet gherkin.

Thinly sliced baked ham with mustard butter.

Baked ham on nut bread spread with tomato butter.

Baked ham with chutney on pumpernickel.

Thin slices of baked ham and smoked salmon with plenty of sweet butter; delicious on heavy black bread.

Thinly sliced baked ham with slivers of white meat of chicken.

Sliced Westphalian-style ham (from any delicacy shop) on thinly sliced white bread.

Chopped ham with English mustard and fresh horse-radish and cream.

Chopped ham with sweet gherkin and a little chopped pineapple.

Chopped ham with chopped ripe olive and grated cheese.

Chopped ham and chopped chicken in equal parts and a few chopped, toasted Brazil nuts mixed with them. Season with English mustard or horse-radish.

Thinly sliced tongue with French mustard.

Thinly sliced tongue with chopped chives.

Thinly sliced tongue with Roquefort butter.

Thinly sliced tongue with grated fresh horse-radish mixed with cream.

Chopped tongue with sweet gherkins and French mustard.

Chopped tongue with chopped Gruyère cheese and mayonnaise.

Thin slices of rare roast beef with plenty of English mustard or horse-radish and cream.

Thin slices of roast lamb with garlic butter.

Chopped lamb with curry butter and chutney.

Slices of roast veal with anchovy butter.

Thinly sliced cold fresh ham with chopped pickled onions.

Cold fresh ham with garlic butter.

Sliced salami with *fines herbes* butter.

Slices of bologna with thin slices of Cheddar cheese.

Tuna-fish paste.

Shrimp spread.

Lobster spread.

Crabmeat mixed with chopped chives and mayonnaise.

Thinly sliced smoked sturgeon.

Smoked salmon with horse-radish.

Anchovy fillets with chopped egg.

Sardine and thinly sliced dill pickle.

Sardine spread.

Sardine and chopped egg and mayonnaise.

Fresh salmon flaked and mixed with mayonnaise and combined with paper thin slices of cucumber.

Thin slices of onion with salt.

Sliced onion marinated in French dressing for several hours and drained.

Sliced onion and cucumber.

Chopped olive and mayonnaise.

Chopped olives and nuts in equal portions bound with cream cheese.

Chopped olive and egg and mayonnaise.

Finely chopped green pepper with a binding of mayonnaise.

Cream cheese and fresh horse-radish.

Cream cheese and chives with cucumber.

Thinly sliced avocado with garlic butter.

Any highly flavored cheese such as Swiss, Gruyère, Brie, Camembert, Limburger, Liederkranz, Oka, aged Cheddar, Gorgonzola, Provolone, Stilton, Cheshire, etc. They are of course much better when served on thin, dark breads that have good round flavor, ryes of all kinds, pumpernickel, and Italian whole wheat.

THE HIGHBALL SANDWICH

The highball sandwich is a coinage of my own, I believe. It has been the solution for many of my friends and pupils who wanted to know what to serve a group of men meeting for an evening of cards or talk, or to a mixed group which was to have highballs during an evening gathering.

It is the larger brother of the cocktail sandwich. It is thicker by an eighth of an inch or so and about three inches square. It fills in when a substantial snack is desired and where a buffet table would be a nuisance. Furthermore, such sandwiches may be prepared or ordered in advance and kept in the refrigerator till they are to be served.

The highball sandwich should nearly always be on dark, well-flavored bread and should be well filled and substantial in appearance. Chicken, meats, and cheese are the most acceptable fillings, with plenty of spice and sauce. The mixtures welcome at cocktail time are not as desirable here nor are the very "gooey" fillings which have a tendency to drip here and there. (Heaven help the hostess who gives men drippy or sliding sandwiches!)

Serve plenty of pickles with these snacks, additional mustard and horse-radish, and some celery and radishes; usually, green onions will be appreciated.

❦ SANDWICHES WITH CHAMPAGNE OR PUNCHES

Here is one place I feel that white bread is a necessity and where one is rather limited in choice of fillings. After all, champagne is the luxury drink to most of us and graces festive occasions better than anything else.

Paper-thin sandwiches of *pâté de foie gras* and white

meat of chicken are the most complementary items to serve. Ham, too, in all its forms, and perhaps cream cheese and chives, if you care for a rather sharp contrast of flavors, as I do. But remember to make the sandwiches thin and tempting and a fitting accompaniment to your beverage.

OPEN-FACE SANDWICHES

These are typically European offerings, for the open face *belegte brotchen* has for years been a standard part of the food service of many European homes. Great platters of open-face slices come into the dining room or drawing room every night to tempt the appetite and to add pounds to the girth—how sad that food should do that to some of us who love it so well!

No article of food served gives the cook more chance to express artistic urges than these bits of fodder to encourage drinking. (I have at times found it necessary to drink in order to drown the flavor of some of the combinations!)

I shall include here a few of my favorites and shall let your imagination do the rest. If you care for the "bewitched" bread, you may set your thinking cap and invent all the combinations your fertile mind will permit.

Use substantial slices of firm bread, for there is nothing quite so unpleasant as flabby bits of bread giving way in your hand and tumbling to the floor. Cut the bread about one quarter to three eighths of an inch thick and spread it with butter. Arrange fillings with care to provide a properly made bed for the decorations, and allow the sandwiches to chill thoroughly before serving.

OPEN-FACE CHICKEN SANDWICH

Spread the bread slice well with sweet butter. Place even slices of cold white meat of chicken on it in an orderly fashion. Sprinkle with chopped, blanched almonds, and decorate with fans made of tiny sweet gherkins sliced very thin almost through and spread out fanwise.

CHICKEN AND HAM OPEN FACE

Spread a round slice of bread well with butter and place a round slice of cold baked ham the same size on it. Spread half of this with French mustard and over that place a crescent-shaped slice of cold chicken. Stuff straws of Switzerland Swiss cheese under the chicken so that they form a sunburst effect on the other half of the ham, and sprinkle with paprika. Edge the chicken slice with a tiny band of parsley chopped very fine.

FOIE GRAS OPEN FACE

Spread a rectangle of white bread with sweet butter and then with *foie gras* so that there is a slight ridge in the center of the slice. Edge with finely chopped toasted Brazil nuts and trim the center ridge with round truffle slices.

LIVER PASTE OPEN FACE

Spread slices of bread, preferably white, with a good liver paste or with a smoked liverwurst. Edge with slices of stuffed olive and garnish with chopped egg yolk.

HAM AND EGG OPEN FACE

Spread a rectangular piece of bread with mustard butter. Cover the slice with a piece of baked ham the same size. Then, in one corner place two slices of hard-boiled egg on two slices of red beet. Fit a tiny fan-shaped slice of ham on the corner so that it covers part of the egg. Repeat this in the opposite corner of the sandwich.

TONGUE AND WATER CRESS OPEN FACE

Spread a round of bread with sweet butter and place tiny sprigs of water cress around the edge so that they extend beyond the rim; top this with trimmed slices of tongue and place a dot of chopped chives in the center.

SALAMI AND CHIVES OPEN FACE

Spread a slice of bread with sweet butter. Place half slices of salami around the edge to give a scalloped effect.

Then spread the center with a cream cheese and chive spread so that it covers most of the sandwich; decorate with chopped parsley and chives or with a line of *fines herbes* butter forced through a pastry tube.

SAUSAGE AND CHEESE OPEN FACE

Spread slices of bread with sweet butter and place two thin slices of sausage on them—salami, bologna, cervelat, or any other type you may desire. Top these with thinly cut radish slices and then a round slice of cheese—Switzerland Swiss or Cheddar. Decorate with strips of pimiento.

SMOKED SALMON OPEN FACE

Spread rounds of bread with sweet butter and then place thin slices of smoked salmon on it. Top the salmon with a slice of unpeeled cucumber and a few grains of red caviar.

TOMATO AND EGG OPEN FACE

Place slices of firm ripe tomato on well-buttered bread slices, top with slices of hard-boiled egg, and garnish with finely chopped chives and curled anchovy fillets.

ROQUEFORT OPEN FACE

Spread slices of bread with Roquefort cheese butter. Edge with a frame of finely chopped chives and decorate with tiny mushroom caps.

ROAST BEEF OPEN FACE

Spread slices of bread with sweet butter and cover with slices of rare roast beef. Decorate with slices of pickled walnuts and pickle fans.

CUCUMBER OPEN FACE

Spread slices of bread with sweet butter. Alternate rows of unpeeled cucumber slices, onion slices, and slices of red beet so that they overlap. Decorate with chopped egg white.

CHOPPED HAM OPEN FACE

Spread slices of bread with sweet butter and well-spiced chopped ham. Decorate with crossbars of cheese strings, green pepper strings, and pimiento strings.

EGG OPEN FACE

Spread round slices of bread with tomato butter. On each place a slice of tomato topped with a cold poached egg well covered with mayonnaise. (For cold poached eggs, you proceed in the usual manner save for leaving the eggs in the boiling water till the yolk is set, but not hard.) Dust the mayonnaise with a few chopped chives.

CHICKEN AND TOMATO OPEN FACE

Spread slices of bread with sweet butter. Cover with slices of white meat of chicken and top with rounds of sliced tomato. Sprinkle bits of crisp bacon over the tomato and garnish with sweet gherkin slices.

AVOCADO OPEN FACE

Spread slices of bread with garlic butter. Place thin slices of avocado alternated with slices of tomato on each slice and sprinkle with chopped chives and parsley. Serve immediately.

SHRIMP OPEN FACE

Spread slices of bread with *fines herbes* butter. Arrange cooked shrimp on them and place a dot of mayonnaise inside the curl of each shrimp. Decorate with chopped egg.

HOT SANDWICHES

These are very satisfactory tidbits to serve with cocktails or late at night with highballs. You definitely need a good staff in the kitchen to do most of these or you must be quick and efficient yourself. They must be served hot and in relays of twelve or fifteen for a group of ten or so people.

This is a nation of hamburger and nutburger fans, so why not have at the next gathering of friends the same thing that attracts so many to the roadside stands? These are everyday foods, but wait! Give them a new importance by making them cocktail size:

COCKTAIL HAMBURGERS

First of all, for these get some tiny rolls; some supermarkets carry them and you will also find there small brown-and-serve rolls. Ideally, you would get your baker to make special rolls for you, I should say about one and one half inches in diameter.

To one pound of chopped sirloin of beef, with as little fat as possible, add two tablespoonfuls of onion juice and two to three tablespoonfuls of heavy cream, a teaspoonful or more of salt, and a teaspoonful of freshly ground black pepper. Mix thoroughly with the fingers and form into tiny cakes, an inch and a quarter in diameter and about one quarter of an inch thick. Sauté them in butter very quickly and place in the heated, buttered rolls and serve with mustard and horse-radish on the plate. I advise you to have plenty of these, for they are popular.

CHICKEN GIBLET SANDWICHES

> 1 *pound of giblets (gizzard, heart, liver)*
> 2 *tablespoonfuls of olive oil*
> 1 *tablespoonful of chopped shallot*
> 1 *teaspoonful of salt*
> 2 *tablespoonfuls of cognac*
>   *thyme, tarragon, parsley*

Chop the giblets very fine. Pour olive oil into an iron skillet and heat over a low flame. Add the chopped shallots, the herbs, and the chopped giblets. Sauté slowly, and lastly, add the salt and the cognac. Spread on slices of toasted bread, top with another slice, and serve at once. To vary this, you may roll the mixture in white bread, secure the roll with a toothpick, and toast under the broiler. Remove the toothpick before serving.

Toasted cheese rolls

> 1 cupful shredded American cheese
> 1 tablespoonful of chili sauce
> 1 teaspoonful each of dry mustard and finely
>   ground black pepper
> ½ teaspoonful of salt
> 2 eggs, beaten

Mix the cheese with the chili sauce and the dry spices; add the well-beaten eggs and mix thoroughly. Spread a little of this mixture on small slices of fresh white bread and roll tightly. Secure with toothpicks and toast under a slow flame. Remove the toothpicks before serving.

Chicken hamburgers

Mix one and one half cupfuls of cooked and chopped chicken with a teaspoonful of chopped parsley and a teaspoonful of chives. Add two teaspoonfuls of dry bread crumbs and enough heavy cream to bind. Form into small cakes, sauté quickly in butter, and serve in small buns as directed for the beef hamburgers.

CREAM CHEESE ROLLS

> 1½　cupfuls of cream cheese
> 1　egg, beaten
> ½　teaspoonful of salt
> 2　tablespoonfuls of chopped chives
> 1　tablespoonful of chopped parsley
> 1　teaspoonful of onion juice

Mix cream cheese, salt, chives, parsley, and onion juice. Mix with beaten egg and beat thoroughly. Spread slices of white bread, well-buttered, with the mixture; roll tightly and secure with toothpicks. Toast under a very low flame till well browned.

HOT MUSHROOM SANDWICH

> 1　cupful of chopped mushrooms
> 2　tablespoonfuls of butter
> 1　tablespoonful of chopped chives
> 1　tablespoonful of chopped parsley
> 1　teaspoonful of Escoffier Sauce Diable
> ½　teaspoonful of salt
> 　cream

Sauté the mushrooms in butter till thoroughly browned. Add the chives, parsley, sauce, and salt. Add just enough cream to bind, spread on slices of hot toast which are well buttered, and top with a second slice. Serve at once.

BACON AND HAZELNUT SANDWICH

Spread slices of hot toast with butter and hazelnut spread. Put slices of crisp bacon and thin slices of tomato on the toast and cover with a well-buttered piece of toast.

ROLLED SANDWICHES

I think rolled sandwiches rightly belong with tea food; but in case you have some particular yearning for them with cocktails, here are some general directions for preparing them: Use fine white bread that is very spongy—experiment with it to see if it has the elasticity to roll without cracking. Spread the squares carefully and roll as tightly as possible. Roll each sandwich in a tiny square of waxed paper and allow to chill thoroughly before serving.

Water cress is one of the most popular fillings for rolled sandwiches and it makes very decorative ones. Other fillings are smoked salmon, tomato butter, *fines herbes* butter, chopped chicken, and chopped ham.

CHAPTER 5

HOT HORS D'OEUVRE
FOR COCKTAIL PARTIES

T HERE ARE PROBABLY more ideas for hot snacks extant than there are toothpicks in a toothpick factory. I have been served under the label of hot hors d'oeuvre everything from a hamburger to a banana fritter. I shall not attempt to cover that many nor that scope, but I shall set down a few of my favorite recipes and augment the list you already have for such occasions.

I think, in order to simplify matters as we go on, it might be wise to list and define some of the terms I shall be using in this chapter.

Allumettes: Tiny fingers of puff paste baked with various toppings.

Barquettes: Tiny pastry shells in the shape of a boat, filled with various things and grilled or baked.

Beignets: French for fritters.

Bouchées: The smallest member of the patty-shell clan. Tiny shells of puff paste which are exceedingly useful and decorative.

Brochettes: Arrangements of meats and vegetables on tiny skewers, grilled or fried for service on the skewer.

Crêpes: Thin pancakes rolled around fillings, or stacked with filling in between and sliced.

Tartlets: Round tarts filled with various savory mixtures, with the mixture as well as the pastry hot.

Hot hors d'oeuvre require plates for each guest, and in some cases it is wise to have forks or tiny spoons also. Naturally, if you are having an elaborate service with various types of hot and cold dishes, you would have these things on your buffet table anyway, and I feel there are certain foods that are unusual enough and delicious enough to warrant the extra bother that additional equipment makes.

For service dishes you will find that any of the usual table service dishes fulfill the requirements for cocktail time; it is a case of getting along with what you have, more than it is a problem of finding special dishes.

However, if you are fortunate enough to have a huge, old-fashioned English breakfast dish of silver or china with a hot-water base you are lucky, for you can serve on it several different dishes at one time and keep them all hot.

If you have a limited number of special serving dishes and still wish to have a variety of hot snacks, use dinner plates. Have them as hot as possible and cover them with a neatly folded napkin. Also, there are available now little hot-plates with alcohol or electric heaters for a nominal sum at any hotel supply house or house-furnishings department. These are exceedingly handy for any type of buffet service; you will find yourself using them often.

For things served *en brochette* you need skewers of either wood or metal. When serving hot *brochettes*, it is best to have plenty of little paper cocktail napkins at hand so that guests can wrap a napkin around the skewer and protect their fingers.

If, however, you are serving just a few hot things before dinner, simply pass them together on a heated plate and have individual plates for guests if they seem necessary. Never bring in individual plates already containing one of this and one of that and one of the other for each guest. One of the joys of this type of food is to have a liberty of choice, to explore unknown territory, and to pick on one's favorites. So give your guests a chance to experiment.

You will find recipes for *feuilletage,* or puff paste, and for flaky pastry, in the chapter on canapés, with instructions on how to make the various pastry forms and shapes.

HOT CANAPÉS

First, here are two basic sauces you will need ocassionally:

BASIC BÉCHAMEL SAUCE *(cream sauce)*

        4 tablespoons of butter
        3 tablespoons of flour
    1½ cups of half cream and half milk
        salt
        freshly ground pepper

Melt the butter and add the flour. Cook until well blended and bubbly. Slowly add the milk and cream, stirring constantly to be sure the mixture does not lump. Continue stirring and cooking until the sauce is smooth and thickened. Season to taste with salt and pepper.

For a slightly thicker and richer sauce, after the sauce is done, put it over hot, not boiling, water and stir in two lightly beaten egg yolks. Cook and stir until smooth and thickened. Do not let the water boil or the sauce will curdle.

MORNAY SAUCE

Add one half cup of grated Parmesan cheese to one and one half cups of Béchamel sauce. Blend thoroughly and cook gently until the cheese melts into the sauce.

SARDINE CANAPÉS

Mash a tin of boneless sardines with the juice of half a lemon and one half teaspoonful of onion juice. When thoroughly mashed, bind with a little mayonnaise and pile on buttered rounds of toast. Top each canapé with a small square of Cheddar cheese and place under a low flame till cheese is melted.

HAM CANAPÉS

Chop three quarters of a cupful of baked ham rather coarsely. Add one half teaspoonful of freshly ground black pepper, a teaspoonful of onion juice, and enough mayonnaise to bind. Pile on rounds of toast and grill very slowly.

HAM AND OLIVE CANAPÉS

> ½ cupful of chopped ham
> ¾ cupful of grated Switzerland Swiss cheese
> ½ cupful of chopped olives
> 1 tablespoonful of chopped onion

Blend the ham and one half cupful of cheese thoroughly. Add the olives and the chopped onion and mix. Pile on buttered toast rounds; sprinkle with remaining grated cheese and place under a low flame till cheese melts.

CHICKEN AND ALMOND CANAPÉS

> ¾ *cupful of chopped chicken*
> ½ *cupful of chopped almonds*
> ¼ *cupful of grated Switzerland Swiss cheese*
> 1 *teaspoonful of chopped gherkin*
> *salt, pepper*
> *mayonnaise to moisten*

Mix the chicken with almonds and grated cheese. Add the gherkin and salt and pepper to taste. If the paste is not bound together, add a little mayonnaise to hold it. Pile on buttered toast rounds and grill under a low flame. You may top this with a slice of blanched almond if you wish.

ASPARAGUS TIP CANAPÉS

Heat some freshly cooked or canned asparagus tips in butter till they are heated through. Place them on fingers of buttered toast, sprinkle well with grated American cheese, and place under the broiler till the cheese is melted. (Cut the asparagus tips down to the size of the toast fingers.)

ANCHOVY CHEESE FINGERS

Arrange anchovy fillets on fingers of buttered toast. Sprinkle with a mixture of Switzerland Swiss and Parmesan cheese, grated. Put under the broiler to melt.

HAM AND CHEESE CANAPÉS

Arrange rounds of sliced baked ham on toast rounds. Sprinkle well with chopped chives, chopped pimiento, and grated Switzerland Swiss cheese. Place under a broiler till the cheese is thoroughly melted.

SHRIMP CANAPÉS

Mix one cupful of chopped shrimp with a tablespoonful of onion juice, two tablespoonfuls of grated Switzerland Swiss cheese, and enough mayonnaise to bind; salt and pepper to taste. Pile on rounds of buttered toast and heat in a moderately hot oven.

ESCARGOT CANAPÉS

>   1 can of imported snails
>   1½ tablespoonfuls of chopped parsley
>   1 shallot, finely chopped
>   pinch of thyme

Chop the snails. Sauté them in two tablespoonfuls of butter in which you have melted the chopped shallot. Add the thyme and the parsley and pile high on rounds of buttered toast.

CURRIED SHRIMP CANAPÉS

Sauté a tablespoonful of chopped onion in two table-spoonfuls of butter. Add one and one half teaspoonfuls of curry powder and a teaspoonful of chutney. Sauté one pound of shrimp in this mixture; place them on rounds of buttered toast and sprinkle with chopped egg white and chopped parsley.

HAM AND SARDINE CANAPÉS

Mix together one half cupful each of chopped ham and mashed sardines. Add a teaspoonful of Escoffier Sauce Diable, two teaspoonfuls of chopped chives, and a table-spoonful of chopped gherkin. Mix these well; pile on rounds of buttered toast; sprinkle with grated American cheese and grill.

EGG AND SARDINE CANAPÉS

Mix two hard-boiled eggs, chopped very fine, and a teaspoonful each of chopped parsley, tarragon, and chives with one half cupful of very thick Béchamel or cream sauce (thickened with egg yolks or arrowroot). Spread buttered toast fingers with this mixture and place a whole boneless and skinless sardine on each one. Sprinkle with a little grated Parmesan cheese and grill under the broiler till browned.

ANCHOVIED CHICKEN LIVER CANAPÉS

Sauté two or three chicken livers in two tablespoonfuls of anchovy butter, or plain butter to which you have added some chopped anchovy fillets or a teaspoonful of anchovy paste. Add a pinch of thyme to the pan as well. When the livers are cooked through, remove from the pan and chop with a teaspoonful each of parsley and chives—chervil, too, if it is available. When thoroughly chopped, blend into a paste with the butter from the pan and a teaspoonful of cognac. Pile on buttered rounds of toast. Heat in the oven a minute or two before serving.

CHICKEN GIBLET CANAPÉS

Use the recipe for chicken giblets in the section on hot sandwiches in the previous chapter. Pile the cooked giblets on rounds of buttered toast and sprinkle with grated Parmesan cheese and put under the broiler to brown.

CRABMEAT CANAPÉS NO. 1

If the Dungeness crabs are available to you, take the leg meat of two crabs, carefully removed whole, and sauté it in three tablespoonfuls of butter to which you have added chopped parsley and chopped chives. When the legs are heated through and nicely browned, arrange them on fingers of well-buttered toast and sprinkle with chopped parsley.

CRABMEAT CANAPÉS NO. 2

Heat one cupful of flaked crabmeat in half a cupful of sauce Mornay (cream sauce to which you have added cheese). Spread on well-buttered rounds of toast, sprinkle with grated Parmesan cheese and chopped parsley, and grill until lightly browned.

ITALIAN CANAPÉS

Spread well-buttered fingers of toast with a spinach purée. Cover with a very heavy sauce Mornay, buttered bread crumbs, grated Parmesan cheese, and chopped chives. Brown under the broiler.

ALLUMETTES

Allumettes, according to their title, should be the size of a match, but they are actually oblongs about one by three inches.

ANCHOVY ALLUMETTES

Cut puff paste into strips about one by three inches. On each strip place a little *fines herbes* butter that has been well flavored with anchovy. Place one or two anchovy fillets on each *allumette,* and bake in a hot oven for ten or fifteen minutes or until well browned.

ALLUMETTES OF CHICKEN AND HAM

Spread strips of puff paste with chicken and ham paste. Place strips of cold chicken and ham on this and sprinkle with buttered crumbs. Bake in a hot oven for ten or fifteen minutes or till browned and cooked through.

ALLUMETTES OF CHEESE

Sprinkle grated Parmesan and Switzerland Swiss cheese on the strips of puff paste. Cover with thin strips of Switzerland Swiss cheese and bake in a hot oven till well browned.

CHICKEN ALLUMETTES

Place a strip of chopped chicken on each *allumette.*
Cover with cooked cocks' combs or bits of sautéed chicken
liver and bake in a hot oven for about fifteen minutes.

BARQUETTES

The tiny boat-shaped pastries I described at the beginning of this chapter should be made of flaky pastry baked
in the tiny boat-shaped pans which you can buy at a hardware store that deals in good kitchen equipment.

CURRIED CHICKEN BARQUETTES

Brown a chopped onion in two tablespoonfuls of butter.
Add two teaspoonfuls of curry powder, a teaspoonful of
chutney, a teaspoonful of chopped nuts, a teaspoonful of
grated coconut, and half a cupful of cream. Thicken this
with a tablespoonful of arrowroot so that it obtains firmness not usually found in a sauce. Chop one cupful of
chicken meat very fine with a few almonds and place a
heaping teaspoonful in each barquette. Cover with the
curry sauce; sprinkle with a little grated coconut and put
under the broiler to glaze.

BARQUETTES OF LOBSTER

> *meat of one cooked lobster of medium size, or one can of lobster meat*
> 1 *onion, chopped fine*
> 2 *tomatoes, peeled and seeded*
> 3 *tablespoonfuls of butter*
> ½ *cupful of white wine*
> *parsley, tarragon, chervil*
> 2–3 *teaspoonfuls of arrowroot for thickening*

Sauté the onion and tomato in butter till they are melted and add the chopped herbs and the white wine. Let these simmer till well blended and if there is not enough moisture, add a little more wine. Salt and pepper to taste and stir in the arrowroot. When thickened, add the lobster which has been picked into small pieces. Let it poach in the sauce till well heated and fill the *barquettes*. Sprinkle with buttered bread crumbs and place under the broiler until browned.

LAMB KIDNEY BARQUETTES

Soak three lamb kidneys in salted water for three hours. Skin, remove the tendons, and chop very fine. Place two tablespoonfuls of butter in an iron skillet, add one shallot, chopped very fine, and brown lightly. Chop one half cupful of mushrooms and add those and the chopped kidneys and a pinch of thyme. Sauté gently till the kidneys are well browned and add one half cupful of heavy cream mixed with two egg yolks. Stir till well thickened and fill the *barquettes*. Sprinkle with buttered crumbs and brown under the broiler.

CLAM BARQUETTES

Heat one can of minced razor clams in a double boiler. Add one half teaspoonful of salt and one half teaspoonful of freshly ground pepper. Add one cupful of heavy cream mixed with the yolks of two eggs and one and one half teaspoonfuls of arrowroot powder. Stir gently till well thickened. Add one tablespoonful of Madeira or sherry. Fill *barquettes* with this mixture, sprinkle with grated Parmesan cheese, and place under the broiler to brown.

ANCHOVY AND MUSHROOM BARQUETTES

Melt two tablespoonfuls of butter in a skillet. Add two tablespoonfuls of chopped onion, six anchovy fillets, chopped fine, and a cupful of chopped mushrooms. Sauté them well till all are thoroughly blended and the onions and mushrooms slightly browned. Mix this well with just enough very heavy cream sauce to bind, and fill the *barquettes* with the mixture. Sprinkle with buttered bread crumbs and place under the broiler to brown.

CRAWFISH BARQUETTES

Place two or three crawfish tails that have been cooked in a well-spiced broth in each *barquette,* and cover with a heavy Mornay sauce. Sprinkle with grated Parmesan cheese and place under the broiler to brown.

BARQUETTES OF HAM

Mix one cupful of chopped baked ham with two tablespoonfuls each of chopped green pepper, chopped olive, and chopped onion. Add one tablespoonful each of chopped parsley and chopped Brazil nuts. Blend these ingredients with two tablespoonfuls of sherry and fill the *barquettes.* Cover with a Béchamel sauce and place under the broiler.

CRABMEAT BARQUETTES

> 1 *cupful of crabmeat, flaked*
> 2 *tablespoonfuls of butter*
> 1 *tablespoonful of chopped onion*
> 2 *tablespoonfuls of chopped celery*
> 1 *teaspoonful each of parsley and chives*
> ½ *cupful of bread crumbs*
> *salt, pepper, tarragon*

Melt the butter in an iron skillet and in it brown the onion, chives, celery, and parsley. Add the crabmeat, bread-

crumbs, and seasonings, and mix well. If it is too dry, add
two tablespoonfuls of heavy cream to bind. Fill *barquettes*
with this mixture, cover with sauce Mornay, and brown
under the broiler.

BACON AND CHEESE BARQUETTES

Fry three or four slices of bacon very crisp; drain and
crush into little bits. Mix with a half cupful of grated
Gruyère cheese and two well-beaten eggs. Salt and pepper
to taste, pour into the *barquette* cases, sprinkle with a little
more grated cheese, and place under the broiler till set.

SHRIMP BARQUETTES

Sauté a pound of shelled raw shrimp in an iron skillet
with two tablespoonfuls of butter, a tablespoonful of
chopped onion, and a tablespoonful of chopped parsley.
Salt and pepper to taste. Add one half cupful of heavy
cream and two egg yolks, and stir till well thickened. Add
a half wineglassful of cognac and fill the *barquette* shells.
Sprinkle with grated Parmesan cheese and buttered crumbs
and place under the broiler.

ᎌBEIGNETS, OR FRITTERS

Below are listed suggestions for many kinds of fritters, each item first to be dipped in the following batter:

FRITTER BATTER

>   2 *cupfuls of flour*
>   4 *tablespoonfuls of butter, creamed*
>   2 *eggs, well beaten*
>   *salt, pepper, nutmeg*
>   1 *cupful of milk*

Mix the flour and the creamed butter and add the eggs. Season to taste, and add enough milk to make a batter the consistency of heavy cream. This should require about one cupful. This batter is much better if made slightly in advance.

The fritters should be fried in deep fat, oil or leaf lard heated to about 380° F. They require about three or four minutes of cooking. Drain them well and serve on a napkin.

VEGETABLE FRITTERS

Marinated buds of cooked cauliflower or raw cauliflower.
Marinated hearts of artichoke, previously cooked.
Tiny marinated onions.
Marinated celery cubes.
Marinated cubes of celery knob.
Marinated mushrooms.
Marinated Brussels sprouts.
Marinated asparagus tips.
Tiny raw tomatoes.

Suggested marinade for vegetables: French dressing made of olive oil and wine vinegar.

FISH FRITTERS

Shrimp cooked in curry sauce.
Lobster cubes that have been marinated in olive oil and sherry.
Crab legs in curry sauce (see the sauce used for curried chicken *barquettes*).
Tiny raw clams.
Canned snails that have been marinated in olive oil and white wine with garlic.

MEAT FRITTERS

Tiny hamburger balls previously browned in butter.

Tiny cubes of sweetbreads previously parboiled and marinated in olive oil and white wine with onion.

Tiny cubes of cold meats, marinated in olive oil and red wine with onion.

POULTRY FRITTERS

Cubes of cold turkey or chicken marinated in oil and lemon juice with tarragon.

Cubes of cold duck marinated in good red Burgundy.

MISCELLANEOUS FRITTERS

Dried prunes puffed in hot water, pitted, and stuffed with tiny sausages which have previously been fried.

Tiny kumquats.

Pickled walnuts.

Small balls of liver paste rolled in chopped toasted Brazil nuts.

Balls of the cheese mixtures (given in the cheese section of the chapter on cold hors d'oeuvre) rolled in chopped nuts.

Remember when you are frying fritters to dip your spoon into the hot fat before you pick up the article to be dipped into the batter. Then, after dipping it into the batter, lower the food tidbit gently into the boiling fat and let it cook for the necessary time.

Fritters should be served with toothpicks handy or with little skewers.

✺ BOUCHÉES

These tiny patty shells are made according to the rule given for puff paste in the canapé chapter.

They are decorative and on the unusual side for cocktail service. They are sturdy finger food, for they have body and are easily popped into the mouth in one piece if the filling is juicy and can be depended upon to hold together if there are two bites.

You may use any of the fillings which were mentioned for the *barquettes,* with this reservation, that everything served in a *bouchée* must be chopped quite fine.

Also, use various creamed meats and fish but make the Béchamel sauce of a good stiff texture which will not run all over the gowns of the ladies and the ties of the gentlemen, not to speak of your own rugs.

Suggestions for *bouchée* fillings:

Creamed chicken to which you have added a little white

wine. Buttered crumbs on top before you brown under the broiler.

Curried shrimp or lobster, using the curry sauce recipe given for fruit curry. Sprinkle with chopped nuts and coconut.

A purée of green peas made by cooking a number of fresh mint leaves and several small white onions with two pounds of fresh peas or one package of frozen ones. Drain, add one eighth of a pound of butter, and force through a fine sieve. Decorate with tiny strips of pimiento.

Chopped chicken livers and gizzards sautéed in butter with chopped onion and parsley. Fill *bouchées* with this mixture, top with a mushroom cap, and brown quickly under the broiler.

SWEETBREAD BOUCHÉES

> *1 pair of sweetbreads, parboiled and skinned*
> *3 tablespoonfuls of butter*
> *½ cupful of chopped mushrooms*
> *⅔ cupful of heavy cream*
> *yolks of 2 eggs*
> *¼ cupful of Madeira*
> *salt, pepper, tarragon, parsley*

Chop the sweetbreads very fine. Melt three tablespoonfuls of butter in a skillet and add sweetbreads and mushrooms with a pinch of fresh tarragon or several leaves of dried tarragon that has been soaked in a little wine to freshen it, and about a tablespoonful of chopped parsley. When the sweetbreads are slightly browned, add the cream that has been well mixed with the egg yolks and stir till smooth and well thickened. Add the Madeira a little at a time and remove from the fire. Fill the *bouchées,* sprinkle with buttered crumbs, and brown under the broiler.

SCALLOP BOUCHÉES

Scallops are a delicious addition to the cocktail menu and one that is welcomed by almost anyone who loves sea food. Try them this way:

> 1½ *cupfuls of scallops, finely chopped*
>   2 *tablespoonfuls of butter*
> ½ *teaspoonful of onion juice*
> ⅔ *cupful of heavy cream*
>   *yolks of 2 eggs*
>   2 *tablespoonfuls of grated Parmesan cheese.*

Sauté the scallops in butter till lightly browned. Salt and pepper to taste and add the onion juice. Stir in the cream mixed with the egg yolk and the grated cheese. When well thickened, remove from the fire; fill the *bouchées,* top with grated cheese, and brown under the broiler.

CROQUETTES

Tiny croquettes are always welcome members of the hors d'oeuvre tray. For this type of service, the croquette mixture should be formed into tiny balls about the size of marbles or into small rolls about one inch long and very thin. Fry them in deep fat at a temperature of about 390° F. (or hot enough to brown a one-inch cube of bread in approximately three quarters of a minute). Drain them well and serve on a napkin.

Usually your meat or fish mixture is mixed with a heavy Béchamel sauce in the proportions given below and the whole blended well and shaped. Dip the croquettes into beaten egg and be sure they are completely submerged. Then dip in bread crumbs and place in a frying basket which previously has been dipped into the hot fat. The average time for frying is about two to three minutes for this size croquette.

CHICKEN CROQUETTES

> 1 *cupful of cooked chicken*
> 1 *teaspoonful of onion juice*
> *few drops of lemon juice*
> 1 *tablespoonful of chopped parsley*
> ¼ *teaspoonful of salt*
> ¼ *teaspoonful of black pepper*
> ⅔ *cupful of sauce, below*

Mix the chicken with seasonings and add the sauce. Allow this to cool, shape into balls, and fry.

BÉCHAMEL SAUCE FOR CROQUETTES

⅓ *cupful of butter*
3 *tablespoonfuls of arrowroot*
1 *cupful of heavy cream*
¼ *teaspoonful of salt*

Use ⅔ cupful of chicken stock and only ½ cupful of cream if you wish. Melt the butter and add the arrowroot, or if this is unavailable, add well-sifted flour. Blend these well and cook for a minute. Stir in the cream and stock gradually and stir with a wire whisk. Once the sauce reaches the boiling point, simmer it for a minute or two.

CHICKEN AND MUSHROOM CROQUETTES

Proceed as for the chicken croquettes except for substituting half a cupful of chopped cooked mushrooms for half the chicken. Omit the onion juice and add one tablespoonful of sherry.

LOBSTER CROQUETTES

1 *cupful of lobster meat, shredded*
1½ *tablespoonfuls of chopped mushrooms*
¼ *teaspoonful of chopped tarragon*
1 *teaspoonful of chopped parsley*
¼ *teaspoonful of salt*
⅔ *cupful of sauce for croquettes*

Mix the lobster, mushroom and seasonings and add the sauce. Cool, form into small balls, and fry.

Variation: Substitute one third cupful of cold cooked rice for one third of the lobster meat and proceed as before.

The same proportions may be used for shrimp or crab-meat croquettes.

MARRON CROQUETTES

Cook twelve chestnuts till tender. Peel them and force through a sieve. Mix with one half teaspoonful of salt, one third teaspoonful of freshly ground pepper, one teaspoonful of chopped parsley, one tablespoonful of melted butter, one tablespoonful of heavy cream, and two well-beaten eggs. Mix thoroughy, form into small balls, and fry. These should be served with chicken croquettes, for they are a nice contrast.

CLAM CROQUETTES

⅔ *cupful of minced razor clams*
½ *cupful of cooked rice*
2 *teaspoonfuls of melted butter*
¼ *teaspoonful of salt*
¼ *teaspoonful of black pepper*
⅔ *cupful of sauce for croquettes*

In making the sauce. substitute clam broth for half the cream. Mix clams, rice and butter and add the seasonings. Mix with enough sauce to bind; form into balls and fry.

CODFISH CROQUETTES

> *1 cupful of cooked, shredded, salt codfish*
> *1½ cupfuls of mashed potatoes*
> *1 teaspoonful of chopped parsley*
> *1 egg, well beaten*
> *½ teaspoonful of ground ginger*
> *½ teaspoonful of black pepper*

Mix the shredded codfish and the mashed potatoes well. Add the seasonings and the well-beaten egg. Form into balls and dip in egg and breadcrumbs and fry.

Variation: The same mixture makes delicious small codfish cakes if you drop it by spoonfuls into a well-buttered skillet and sauté until a delicate brown.

Also delicious made with cooked finnan haddie or kippered herring.

BEEF CROQUETTES

> *1 cupful of chopped roast beef*
> *1 teaspoonful of Escoffier Sauce Diable*
> *½ teaspoonful of salt*
> *1 teaspoonful of onion juice*
> *1 teaspoonful of dry mustard*
> *½ cupful of sauce for croquettes*

Mix the beef well with seasonings and add the sauce Mold into small rolls and fry.

CORNED BEEF BALLS

>1½ *cupfuls of corned beef hash (canned or from*
>   *your own recipe)*
>1 *teaspoonful of chopped chives and parsley*
>1 *teaspoonful of chili sauce*
>1 *egg, well-beaten*

Mix the corned beef hash with the seasonings and add the well-beaten egg. Mold into balls and dip in egg and crumbs and fry.

HAM CROQUETTES

>1 *cupful of ham, finely chopped*
>1 *teaspoonful onion juice*
>2 *tablespoonfuls of grated Switzerland Swiss cheese*
>1 *teaspoonful of tomato sauce*
>1 *tablespoonful of chopped olive*
>½ *cupful of sauce for croquettes*

Mix the ham and seasonings and add the sauce. Blend well, form into balls, dip in egg and crumbs, and fry.

CHEESE CROQUETTES

> 2 *eggs, separated*
> ½ *cupful bread crumbs*
> 1 *cupful of grated American cheese*
> 1 *cupful of grated Swiss cheese*
> ½ *teaspoonful each of salt and dry mustard*
> 1 *tablespoonful of Escoffier Sauce Diable*

Separate the eggs and beat the whites very stiff. Mix the yolks and seasonings and add to the bread crumbs. Mix well with the grated cheese and fold in the whites of egg. Form into balls or sticks, dip in egg and crumbs, and fry.

SMALL PASTIES

These are made with a puff paste or *feuilletage* and should be enchanting to look at and delicious to taste. They are not reducing, so think well before you eat three or four of them. And don't serve them too often!

Roll out a sheet of puff paste quite thin and cut tops out of it with a fluted, round pastry cutter. Choose any size you desire, but remember they are eaten from the fingers; don't go over an inch and one half or two inches in diameter.

Next roll out the paste again a bit thinner and cut the bottoms. Place them on a baking sheet, put a bit of the filling about the size of a nut on each piece and cover with the tops. Fit the two together neatly and press together around the edge so that the pasty is well shaped and tightly secured. Brush with egg or milk and bake in a hot oven about twelve to fifteen minutes.

Suitable fillings for pasties:

Small patties of ground, lean cooked pork mixed with salt, thyme, pepper, and just a touch of dry mustard. One half pound of ground pork should make about ten pasties.

Chopped chicken. One cupful of chopped chicken with a tablespoonful each of chopped parsley, chives, and egg yolk. Add one teaspoonful of chopped tarragon, and bind with creamed butter.

Anchovy. Spread the bottom crust with some anchovy butter and place two or three rolled anchovy fillets on it. Cover and press together.

Chicken giblets. Sauté chopped livers, giblets, and hearts, and cocks' combs if you like them, about one and one half cupfuls in all, in two tablespoonfuls of butter. Add one half teaspoonful of salt, a tablespoonful each of chopped chives and parsley, and a few sprigs of tarragon. Add one half cupful of chicken broth mixed with a teaspoonful of arrowroot and let it thicken slightly.

Beef pasties. Sauté three tablespoonfuls of chopped onion and a clove of garlic, well chopped, in two tablespoonfuls of butter. Add one-half pound of chopped, tender beef and brown well. Season with a teaspoonful of salt, some freshly ground black pepper and a few leaves of thyme. Bind this with one half cupful of double-rich broth or with a small quantity of brown sauce.

Snails. A whole canned snail, sprinkled with chopped parsley and shallot and dotted with butter, makes an unusual and toothsome bite baked into a pasty.

TURNOVERS

Turnovers may be made with puff paste or with a plain pastry according to your own taste. I think the most inviting ones are the semicircular variety made by cutting out a large circle of dough and doubling it over. Brush with egg and bake in a hot oven from ten to fifteen minutes. They may be made with any chopped meat filling you may desire, highly seasoned of course; or any fish filling.

May Massee, the New York editor of many delightful children's books, always serves tiny turnovers made with rolled anchovy fillets that are to be found bottled, everywhere, and these turnovers are very popular with her guests.

Grated American cheese, about one cupful mixed with two tablespoonfuls of Escoffier Sauce Robert, or with a good chili sauce and a bit of onion juice and a teaspoonful of dry mustard, makes a delightful and easy filling for turnovers.

For another, cut circles of paste three to four inches in diameter and spread the surface well with a mixture of one tablespoonful of French mustard mixed with one teaspoonful of dry mustard and a few drops of Worcestershire sauce. On each round place a cocktail frankfurter or a two-inch slice of a large frankfurter and fold over.

Another very flavorful turnover is made from one cupful of chopped smoked tongue mixed with one tablespoonful each of chopped onion, horse-radish and parsley. Bind this if necessary with a little sour cream.

This is a particularly pleasant fish turnover, for the smoky flavor of the haddock seems to be a welcome one at cocktail time: Sauté one and one half cupfuls of choice finnan haddie, which has been flaked first, in two table-spoonfuls of butter with a little chopped parsley. Add one half cupful of chopped cooked mushrooms, and mix it all with one cupful of heavy cream sauce to which you have added two tablespoonfuls of grated Parmesan cheese. Drop by spoonfuls on rounds of pastry and sprinkle with more Parmesan before folding. Pinch the edges and bake in hot oven (400° F.) until delicately browned and crisp.

Whole sardines placed on pieces of pastry and sprinkled with lemon juice, chopped parsley, and chopped onion before folding over make delicious hot turnovers.

One cupful of chopped cold chicken or veal mixed with one half cupful of curry sauce and one tablespoonful of chutney makes a very good filling.

Mash well the contents of a seven-ounce can of tuna fish. Add two tablespoonfuls of chopped hard-boiled egg, and one tablespoonful each of chopped parsley, olives, and chives. Sprinkle with a little lemon juice and a few grains of freshly ground black pepper. Place a tiny dot of butter on each mound before folding over the paste.

Our old standby, ham, takes a little different form here for a change: Mix one half cupful of dry bread crumbs with one teaspoonful of dry mustard, one half teaspoonful of onion juice, two teaspoonfuls each of finely chopped Brazil nuts and chopped raisins, a pinch of thyme, and enough Madeira or sherry to make a stiff paste. Spread this on three slices of cold baked ham and roll as tightly as possible. Cut in two-inch lengths and place on rounds of pastry. Fold and pinch together.

Spread rounds of pastry with a good pâté mixed with butter. Place on this a tablespoonful of chopped chicken first moistened with a little broth flavored with tarragon and white wine. Dot with butter and fold.

One half cupful each of finely chopped cold chicken and ham and grated Switzerland Swiss cheese are blended with a teaspoonful of French mustard and one of onion juice. Moisten with a tablespoonful of tomato sauce and place on rounds of pastry.

Sprinkle rounds of pastry with grated Parmesan cheese. On each piece place a square of filleted kippered herring. Dot with butter, sprinkle with freshly ground pepper and chopped parsley, and fold.

❧ TARTLETS

The Switzerland Swiss Cheese Association, Inc., of New York once published a very interesting cookbook compiled by a number of great Swiss chefs. It is one of the most complete things of its kind, unfortunately not available in English.

I am including several recipes from that book which I feel are unusual and delicious. I ate these dishes first at a delightful party in the Cheese Cellar, at the 1939 New York World's Fair, and determined to get the recipes for this book. I had the dishes both hot and cold, and found them satisfying both ways.

CHEESE TARTLETS NO. 1

  flaky pastry
 4 *eggs*
 6 *ounces of grated Switzerland Swiss cheese*
 1 *teaspoonful of flour*
 ⅔ *cupful of milk*
 ½ *teaspoonful of salt*
 ¼ *teaspoonful each of pepper and nutmeg*

Roll the pastry quite thin and fill tartlet shells or small muffin tins with the paste. Flute the edges with a cutter and prick the bottom of each shell with a fork. Beat the eggs slightly and add the cheese, flour, milk, and seasonings. Stir till well mixed and fill the tartlet shells two thirds full. Bake from twelve to fifteen minutes in a hot oven (425° F.).

CHEESE TARTLETS NO. 2

Line tartlet shells with pastry, flute the edges, and prick the paste. Into each shell put about one heaping teaspoonful of grated Switzerland Swiss cheese (this will vary according to the size of the tartlet shell), and cover with the following mixture:

Mix two thirds cupful of milk, one half cupful of heavy cream, three eggs, a pinch of paprika, and salt and pepper to taste till the ingredients are well blended. Pour over the cheese mixture till shells are two thirds filled. Bake in a hot (450° F.) oven till the tarts are a deep yellow color. Serve very hot.

AUNT LIZZIE'S BACON TART

When I was a child, I spent many summers in a quiet spot on the shores of the Pacific Ocean. With the enthusiasm of childhood and the manifold attractions of the seashore I developed a Gargantuan appetite. I had a Scotch friend who often fed me huge bacon-and-egg tarts, which seemed then to be the most savory and succulent morsels in the world. Since that time, I have put this recipe into party clothes and it has become a popular item whenever I have people in for a party.

> 6 eggs
> 8 slices of bacon
>   salt, pepper, mustard
> 6 tablespoonfuls of milk
> 1 teaspoonful of chopped onion
> 2 tablespoonfuls of chopped parsley
>   flaky pastry

Fry the bacon till crisp, drain, and break into small pieces. Sauté the onion in a little of the bacon fat. Beat the eggs and add the milk, parsley, and seasoning to taste. Lastly, add the onion and bacon pieces and mix thoroughly.

Line the tart shells with flaky pastry and fill with the egg mixture. Bake in a moderate (350° F.) oven till the mixture is well set and serve very hot.

HAM TARTS

> 1½ cupfuls of chopped cooked ham
>   2 tablespoonfuls of olive oil
>   1 tablespoonful of chopped onion
>   2 tomatoes, seeded and diced
>   ½ cupful of chopped olives
>   1 clove of garlic, crushed
>   1 tablespoonful of chopped green pepper
>   salt, pepper, cloves
>   1 tablespoonful of chopped parsley
>   thyme, tarragon
>   flaky pastry
>   topping, below

Heat the olive oil in an iron skillet and brown the onion in it. Add the tomatoes, olives, garlic, and pepper and let this simmer for twenty minutes. Then add the spices and a pinch of leaf thyme and a pinch of leaf tarragon. The ham is added to this sauce and allowed to simmer till it is well saturated with the flavors.

Fill the tart shells, which have been made of flaky pastry and baked, with this mixture and pack firmly. Top with the following:

Beat two eggs well. Make a paste by folding in one cupful of grated Parmesan cheese and one teaspoonful of salt. Top each tart with a tablespoonful of this mixture and place under a low flame till the eggs are set and the tops nicely browned.

HORS D'OEUVRE EN BROCHETTE

This is a substantial service and one that should be exceedingly popular after a football game or skating. Men go for this type of food and you will be blessed as a bountiful host if you appease ravenous appetites this way.

Use plates and forks, the bread-and-butter size plate and any small fork. And have plenty of paper cocktail napkins around to use as a protection for the fingers and to save the good linen cocktail napkins.

Nothing in the world could be as welcome on a cold day after a brisk ride or a football game with a good cocktail or highball.

BEEFSTEAK EN BROCHETTE

Alternate small cubes of good, tender steak and tiny white onions on a small skewer. Your butcher will gladly cut your steak into cubes for you; it should be a good sirloin or tenderloin cut. Let the cubes marinate in olive oil for about two hours before they are to be cooked. Remove from the oil and thread on the skewers. Place under a hot flame and brown very quickly on all sides. Salt and pepper them well and rush them to your guests on a hot plate. I assure you they will disappear like snow in the desert.

A plate of paper-thin slices of bread and butter could accompany this, and have various sauces arranged on your table for those who must gild the lily.

SHISH KEBAB FOR COCKTAILS

Arrange tiny cubes of lean lamb on a skewer with tiny, white onions and small tomatoes if they are in the market, or small slices of tomato. Broil these till nicely browned, season them, and arrange on a hot plate.

KIDNEY AND LAMB EN BROCHETTE

Alternate cubes of lean lamb, small pieces of lamb kidney, and tiny mushroom caps on small skewers. Broil under a medium flame till nicely browned. Season to taste and serve on a hot plate.

CHICKEN LIVERS EN BROCHETTE

Cut chicken livers into small pieces and wrap in thin slices of bacon. Arrange nicely on small skewers and broil. Marinate the livers in Escoffier Sauce Diable for twenty minutes or so before wrapping them if you so desire.

SEAFOOD EN BROCHETTE

Choose small oysters and scallops at your fish market. Wrap the oysters in thin slices of bacon and the scallops in thinly sliced strips of ham. Alternate oysters and scallops on skewers and broil till well browned.

Smoked oysters may be substituted for fresh ones if you so desire.

KIDNEYS AND MUSHROOMS EN BROCHETTE

Cut lamb kidneys into small cubes and brown them very quickly in butter into which you have put a clove of crushed garlic. Place a cube of kidney between two small mushroom caps so that it makes a small ball shape. Place two or three of these on skewers and broil until the mushrooms are browned. Salt and pepper to taste.

✳MISCELLANEOUS HOT SNACKS

LIVER STRUDEL ROLLS

The following recipe is one of the many created by Nata Lee, who was one of the more unusual caterers in New York. She was truly a food stylist, for not only did she know good food, but she always used her imagination to develop ideas which were not only smart but practical as well.

Paste
>   ¼ *pound of sweet butter*
>   ¼ *pound of cream cheese*
>   ¼ *pound of flour*

Work into a dough with the fingers. Chill thoroughly and roll out very thin.

Filling
>   1 *medium large onion, chopped fine and browned in*
>   2 *tablespoons of chicken fat with*
>   ¼ *green pepper*
>   1 *stalk celery*
>   ¼ *pound of calf's liver, diced*
>   *whites of 2 hard-boiled eggs*

Put entire mixture through the meat grinder. Cool, and season to taste. Cut the dough into three-inch squares and place a pencil-shaped roll of the liver mixture on each square. Roll, seal with unbeaten egg white, chill, and bake at 450° F. for about twenty minutes.

KIBBI

For the inventive, imaginative cook, international dishes present a constant and stimulating challenge. Here is a national dish of Iraq and one that makes an ideal hot hors d'oeuvre. You will serve this again and again once you hear the opinion of your guests.

Take two pounds of lean lamb, cut from the leg or the shoulder, and put it through the fine grinder twice. Place the meat in a wooden mixing bowl and salt it well, about two teaspoonfuls. Knead the meat with your hands until it is a firm paste. Run an onion through the grinder to get out all the bits of meat that are left and mix this into the meat paste.

Soak three quarters of a pound of cracked wheat in water for ten minutes and wash thoroughly under running water. Add salt and pepper to this, about one teaspoonful of each, and then mix with the lamb with your hands.

Put this mixture through the fine grinder again and mix it again with your hands.

Pour melted butter into a rectangular baking pan and cover the entire surface of the pan with it. Take about half the lamb mixture and cover the bottom of the pan with it, pressing it down well with the hands.

Brown one and one half cups of diced lamb and about three quarters of a cup of chopped onion in butter and spread this over the layer of lamb paste. Add a couple of handfuls of pine nuts. Cover this with another layer of the paste and cut in squares. Over this pour a cupful of melted butter and bake in a moderate (325° F.) oven till it has cooked through, thirty to forty-five minutes. Cut in small squares and serve very hot.

HAMBURGER BALLS

To one pound of chopped lean sirloin add two table-spoonfuls of onion juice, a small clove of garlic, minced and crushed, and two tablespoonfuls of heavy cream. Mix well and form into tiny balls the size of marbles. Fry very quickly in butter and season to taste. Serve on toothpicks.

NUTBURGER BALLS

Proceed as above except for adding three quarters of a cupful of chopped walnuts to the mixture.

SAUSAGE BALLS

To one pound of ground, fresh pork add two teaspoon-fuls of salt, a teaspoonful of freshly ground black pepper, some finely chopped thyme and sage, and a few grains of cayenne. Form into small balls and fry slowly in a little butter.

CRABMEAT ROLLS

Take large sections of fresh crabmeat and marinate them for two hours in olive oil, a little vinegar, and salt and pepper with a crushed clove of garlic in the dish. Drain the crabmeat well, wrap bits of it in thin strips of bacon or raw ham, and broil the rolls. Serve on toothpicks.

You may use this same method for lobster cubes or shrimp.

OLYMPIA BISCUITS

If you are in a part of the country where you can procure small oysters, the following will prove a popular dish on your menu. I have always made it with the Olympia oysters from Puget Sound and they are ideal for it.

Dip two dozen oysters in egg and bread crumbs and fry them in butter, very quickly. Salt and pepper them well, sprinkle with a little lemon juice and chopped parsley, and place each oyster in a tiny hot baking-powder biscuit which has been split and buttered.

BROILED OYSTERS AND BACON

Jeanne Owen serves this next delicious oyster hors d'oeuvre very often and the demand usually far exceeds the supply. Of course you'll need oyster forks and small plates for these.

For a dozen freshly opened oysters that are left on the half shell, you will need the following: Put three tablespoonfuls of Escoffier Sauce Diable in a small skillet with a minced and crushed garlic clove and three tablespoonfuls of chopped parsley. Heat this very slowly over a low flame.

On each oyster, place about one teaspoonful of pulverized crisp bacon, a small spoonful of the sauce, and a tiny strip of raw bacon. Place under the broiler till the bacon has cooked and the oysters are heated through. Serve at once.

BROILED OYSTERS FINES HERBES

On each oyster left on the half shell place a teaspoonful of *fines herbes* butter. Sprinkle with buttered crumbs and a little grated Switzerland Swiss cheese and place under the broiler till browned.

CHEESE PUFFS

Melt two tablespoonfuls of butter in a saucepan and add one cup of water and one half teaspoonful of salt. When the water boils, add gradually one cupful of sifted flour. Stir this constantly till it makes a thick, smooth batter which will not adhere to the sides of the pan or to the spoon. Remove this from the fire and cool. Then add, a little at a time, three well-beaten eggs and one cupful of grated American cheese. Have oil heated in a deep fat fryer to 390° F. (until a square of bread browns in one minute). Dip the cheese batter into the frying basket in small spoonfuls, always dipping the spoon in the fat before dipping into the batter. Fry until golden brown and drain well on paper towels.

STUFFED MUSHROOM NO. 1

Poach one half pound of any white fish in a little water to which you have added a slice of lemon, a few peppercorns, some parsely, and salt. When it is cooked through and drained, flake it and remove all bones. Mix it with one egg, well-beaten, a tablespoonful of chopped parsley, a teaspoonful of salt, and a little white wine. Fill mushroom caps with this mixture, sprinkle with buttered crumbs and chopped parsley, and brown under the broiler.

STUFFED MUSHROOMS NO. 2

Sauté one half cupful of finely chopped veal or lamb kidney in two tablespoonfuls of butter with one tablespoonful of chopped shallot or chives. Mix this with one half cupful of finely pulverized crisp bacon and one egg, well-beaten. Add a tablespoonful of Madeira. Fill mushroom caps with this mixture, sprinkle with buttered crumbs, and brown under the broiler.

CROQUE MONSIEUR WITH BRIOCHE

Slice *brioche* in slices about one eighth of an inch thick. Spread with butter, and on half of them put a thin slice each of ham, chicken, and Switzerland Swiss cheese. Cover with another piece of *brioche,* dip in beaten egg and milk as you would for French toast and sauté quickly in butter till nicely browned on both sides. Serve very hot.

This same process may be used substituting anchovy fillets for the chicken.

COCKTAIL CRÊPES

These are thin, rolled pancakes with savory fillings. They are attractive as well as delicious. Or, instead of rolling them, you may stack them with filling in between and then slice the stack.

> ⅞ cup of flour
>   pinch of salt
> 3 eggs
> 2 tablespoonfuls of Cognac
> 4 tablespoonfuls of melted butter
>   milk

Beat the eggs and combine with the flour, salt, Cognac, and butter. Add just enough milk to make a smooth batter the consistency of heavy cream. Let the batter stand an hour or so before cooking.

Cook the pancakes one at a time in a tiny skillet. Heat butter in the skillet until bubbly and pour in just enough batter to spread over the bottom of the pan. Tilt the skillet to let the batter run evenly. When the crêpe is brown on the bottom, turn it over to brown the other side. Keep warm in a very low oven until all the crêpes are cooked.

Spread with filling and roll; or spread with filling, stack, and slice.

Unless these are made very small and the fillings are very firm, you will need forks and plates for this service.

Suggested fillings for crêpes:

Diced chicken and sliced blanched almonds in a thick Béchamel sauce.

Chopped mushrooms in a thick Béchamel sauce.

Shrimps or lobster in a thick curry sauce.

Spread each crêpe with *foie gras* and sprinkle with a few chopped pistachio nuts and roll.

Sautéed chopped chicken giblets bound with a little heavy cream.

Add two thirds of a cupful of grated Gruyère cheese to one cupful of heavy Béchamel sauce. Roll in pancakes.

Caviar and sour cream.

Diced ham or tongue in a heavy meat sauce flavored with Madeira.

CHAPTER 6

ACCESSORIES

By ACCESSORIES for cocktail food I do not mean pink and
green potato chips, or colored breads, or anything tricky or
"precious." I mean well-chosen products which enhance
the enjoyment of the more important foods you are serving
and the additional items which may be included in a cocktail party menu to make it more elastic in scope.

NUTS, PICKLES, AND CHIPS

I suppose that of all the many cocktail accessories nuts are probably the most popular, and rightly so, for their texture and rich flavor complements wines and liquors of all sorts. Peanuts, filberts, pistachios, Brazil nuts, walnuts, almonds, all have their place with drinks and may be found, good and bad, everywhere. Macadamia nuts from Honolulu have recently joined this family and a welcome addition, too; they have an unusual flavor and texture not to be found in any other nut. They are everywhere today in the shops in vacuum-packed jars, salted and ready for use.

Brazil nuts are one of the most delicious of all nuts and probably one of the most neglected. They happen to be a particular favorite of mine and I use them in many ways. One of my most memorable taste treats was the first time I ever sampled Brazil-nut chips and was delighted with them. I pass along this pleasant experience in the hope that I may make more Brazil-nut enthusiasts. The recipe has given me a great deal of personal pleasure and satisfaction.

SALTED BRAZIL NUT CHIPS

Slice Brazil nuts lengthwise as thinly as possible. Arrange in a shallow baking pan, adding two tablespoonfuls of butter for every pound of nuts. Sprinkle with salt and toast in a moderate (350° F.) oven, stirring occasionally, until brown. This should take about twenty-five or thirty minutes.

To slice Brazil nuts easily, cover with cold water, bring to a boil, and simmer from three to five minutes. Cool slightly and slice.

SALTED NUTS

If you wish to salt nuts for your cocktail parties or for gift packages, the following instructions are standard for all types of nuts. I think that almonds (and try to get the Jordan variety used in making the famous candy-coated almonds) are universally popular. Blanch them by covering with boiling water and allowing them to stand two or three minutes, then rub off the skin and dry the nuts.

If you are salting peanuts, buy the raw peanuts and skin them by rubbing with the fingers or a linen towel. You will find that home-salted peanuts are a new sensation, for they seem to achieve exceptional flavor when they are slowly toasted in butter. For this, take a half pound of butter to each pound of nuts and cook them slowly in an iron skillet over a low flame. Stir them constantly till they are a golden brown. Drain the nuts on brown paper or paper towels and sprinkle with salt.

For almonds, pistachio nuts, filberts, walnuts, pecans,

and so on, you may use the above method or you may
spread the nuts on a baking sheet and add three tablespoonfuls of butter to each pound of nuts and toast them slowly
in a moderate (350° F.) oven, stirring them often. Sprinkle
with salt and just a tiny bit of cayenne pepper.

Olives are another standard accessory for the cocktail
party, though they are very seldom served correctly. Especially the ripe and green ripe, and other types as well, are
much more delicious when served at room temperature
rather than iced.

Ripe and green ripe olives of all types are enhanced by
the addition of olive oil and a little garlic. True, some of
the green ripes come in a dill sauce, which makes this un-
necessary, but for all the others the dressing is needed. You
will find then the true olive flavor. We are fortunate in
having such superb olives grown in our own country, and
we need never worry about being deprived of them as long
as there is still a California. If you have not tried the dried
olives and the various pickled and spiced ones found in
some of the foreign grocery shops, make a tour, and serve
them next time. You will find new olive flavors and ideas
for arranging a most attractive tray of six or seven different
types always welcome at any cocktail party. The Greeks,
Italians, Syrians, Armenians, all the Mediterranean peo-
ples, have different types of olives so that you may offer a
large assortment.

Pickles, too, are a welcome member of the hors d'oeuvre
table. There are many kinds from which to choose, but if

you stick to the sweet and spiced ones, and the many varieties of dill pickles to be found on most grocery shelves, you will be wise. Pickled onions, too, are on the desirable list and pickled crabapples, prunes, California pickled walnuts, and preserved and pickled melon rinds. If you are fortunate enough to have your own home-made products, don't hesitate to bring them forth. Good home picklers are rare these days and should parade their wares.

Try a large tray arranged nicely with various pickles, olives, and raw vegetables and see if it is not a success.

POTATO CHIPS

Potato chips are popular, I know, but, as with most commercial salted nuts, there is a preponderance of inferior brands on the market, so I feel it is much better to leave them alone than to use the average varieties available. If, however, you know a good brand, use them, heating briefly before serving. If you wish to take the trouble and make your own shoestring or lattice potato chips, that is another matter. They are delicious and popular with anyone.

You need a slicer for thin potato chips or lattice potatoes, and a great deal of patience for shoestrings. All three should be soaked in ice water for ten minutes before frying and should be dried thoroughly before being plunged into the hot fat.

It is a matter of choice whether you use two frying vessels or one. It is probably easier to have two pans of fat (use good oil or leaf lard), one heated to about 250° F. and the other to 400° F. Put the basket with the prepared potatoes into the lower temperature till they are a light brown and transfer to the hot fat to crisp them. Drain potatoes on brown paper or other absorbent (paper towels are perfect for this) and sprinkle with salt and freshly ground black pepper.

❧ BISCUITS

(Crackers in America)

There are literally thousands of varieties of biscuits on the market for service with cocktails or wines. For years and years the imported biscuits were the only ones worthy of the name, but in recent years the American bakers have brought forth several really excellent varieties, all of which may be depended upon for flavor and texture. The thin English water biscuits still remain the most desirable of that type, especially those that are sent from Tunbridge Wells, but for other kinds of biscuits, or crackers, you may trust your local shops and the American bakers.

If you are on a diet (worse luck) you will find a large assortment of low-caloried crackers which you may eat with a clear conscience, for American manufacturers have been quick to sense the need for dietary food items and have profited by it.

Water biscuits for cheese, with the addition of some crusty French bread for those who prefer it, small savory-flavored biscuits of various types (poppy seed, sesame seed, etc.) to be eaten with drinks may all be arranged attractively on your cocktail table, on a combination tray, or in small dishes placed together as a unit. Have several varieties, for there are many people who prefer a dry biscuit to anything else and they too should be catered to. Besides, such biscuits may be kept for several weeks in tin boxes without growing stale. Freshen before serving by heating briefly in the oven.

From Honolulu came the idea for the coconut chip, which was once exotic and is now commonplace. They are smooth and delicious in flavor and not of a greasy texture. The many other knick-knacks and ideas for cocktails which are continually coming on the market are too numerous to mention here. There are various trade-marked tidbits, some good, some bad, coming and going, and if you are an alert shopper you not only keep informed of the new ones but may discover some truly excellent additions for your pantry. Among the best things to have caught on over the years are the cheese-stuffed biscuits from Holland. Visit the shops often, experiment, and you will probably find many things to intrigue your guests.

STRETCHING THE COCKTAIL PARTY

As I mentioned earlier, the cocktail table often includes things which lean toward the buffet supper, and rightly so. Many times a cocktail party stretches out until late; or you have certain friends you wish to stay on and chat, after other guests are gone. Or you are giving a party in a suburban or country house and want to give your guests, who drive a long distance to see you, something more than the regular party food. For any of these occasions, you may stretch the menu and fill in with more substantial dishes.

I know one successful host who always has a large standing roast of beef, perfectly roasted and glazed, and a huge roast turkey on the buffet table at his cocktail parties. These roasts are carved in paper-thin slices and eaten with thin bread and butter, or in tiny pastry snacks. I feel there is a great deal to be said for this.

At another home I know, there is always found as an accessory to the cocktail table a choice ham, baked in claret or Madeira; sometimes hot, sometimes cold. Cold glazed tongue, roast goose, and cold beef à la mode are other dishes which find their way to the cocktail buffet in some homes.

At one time the popularity of smoked turkey almost threatened to extinguish other substantial cocktail food. If you can find the right one, smoked turkey is a delicious food; but beware of buying it blindly, for there are some very inferior birds on the market. And remember, too, that smoked turkey is very rich and should never be carved carelessly. Paper-thin slices are the thing for this delicacy.

If you do except people to stay on and want to have a hot dish to supplement the party food, be sure it is something which will not spoil in standing. Have it prepared in the morning of the party day. Your cook, particularly if *you* are the cook, has enough to do without preparing additional dishes at the last moment.

Lobster, chicken, crabmeat, shrimp, or most any type of fish or meat salad may have a place on the buffet table for an elaborate cocktail party. If you are having a selection of cold meats and sausage as hors d'oeuvre, a bowl of well-seasoned potato salad makes a savory addition.

You have ample leeway to make your table as elaborate or as simple as you wish. Remember this with your cocktail parties and your tables: These are gay affairs; keep up with the spirit of the occasion. The most important key to the success of a cocktail party is the attitude of the hosts. Things should be arranged so that there are no worries on the guests' arrival, and no misgivings about the amount of food in the refrigerator or the amount of liquor in the cellar. True hospitality means that the host is giving his undivided attention to his guests and enjoying the party. No one can feel at home with a worried host. So keep up a steady happy attitude no matter what happens and if there are worries, keep them in the back of your head and don't give them away to anyone else.

❧ THE SOFT DRINKS

I have repeated several times that one should respect the desires of those who do not drink alcohol. Somewhere in the living room have a tray or table arranged with fruit juice of some kind, in an iced pitcher, with glasses and perhaps one of the cola drinks or ginger ale; also, a pitcher of ice water with glasses. These are all thoughtful additions to a party. And don't hide these "accessories" so that people who want soft drinks have that peculiar feeling we once experienced sneaking into a speakeasy. And let us once and for all boycott that strange concoction known as "punch" and take our fruit juice straight. Good, plain, chilled orange or grapefruit juice, tomato juice, grape or pineapple juice will always find customers.

❧ THE TEA TABLE

If you have a large enough establishment to have two tables in your living room, or if your cocktail service can be managed with trays (I am speaking, of course, of a large party) you will be smart to have a beautifully appointed tea table in addition to the cocktail service. For a large affair the tea table is usually set up in the dining room and cocktail service is carried on from a table in the living room. Tea, coffee, sandwiches, thin bread and butter, and various cakes should be on the tea table. And be sure the woman who presides at it has charm and poise and knows most of the guests.

If you have a small place, a tea tray may be arranged on a small table in the same room as the cocktail service. It can be as simple or as elaborate as the dictates of your home make it, but no matter how tea is served be sure that it is well seasoned with hospitality.

CHAPTER 7

HORS D'OEUVRE AS
A FIRST COURSE
AT LUNCHEON OR DINNER

W HILE I ENJOY THE FOODS of all countries, I admit to a partiality to French food at its best, especially sitting on a terrace with a splendid view or along the banks of one of those silvery, winding rivers that give the French countryside such a freshness. With some nostalgia, I recall many happy luncheons in France when trays of beautifully arranged and deliciously prepared hors d'oeuvre were brought to me.

It used to be the custom to serve cold hors d'oeuvre before luncheon and hot hors d'oeuvre before dinner. But that has changed. Hors d'oeuvre in the grand style are no longer common, but the delightful habit of serving *some* hors d'oeuvre, hot or cold, has become more and more universal.

I want to mention the various things which went into the service I once had at the French Pavilion restaurant, for it was probably more typical of pre-war France than any other service in America. Those at my table were offered many trays of smart oblong glass dishes attractively garnished and holding:

Vegetables cooked with olive oil and herbs and seasoned with spices and vinegar and marinades of various sorts. Some were served under a mayonnaise. There were eggplant, zucchini, and celery root, the latter shredded and served with a remoulade sauce. Cauliflower buds, cooked, marinated, and topped with mayonnaise; beet root in a tart sauce; tiny carrots cooked and marinated; cucumber cooked with herbs and olive oil and seasoned magnificently; tiny green beans in a delicious sauce of oil and freshly chopped herbs; onions cooked in a sweet-sour sauce with raisins. Then we were served a raw cucumber salad with a delicately flavored French dressing; thinly sliced tomatoes with a piquant sauce; radishes; a potato salad, a mixed vegetable salad; artichoke bottoms stuffed with a meat farce, marinated, and cooked in the marinade. There were mushrooms, too, and capers, exquisitely subtle in flavor.

The tray included tiny slivers of sausage; bits of brawn (head cheese); a variety of sardines; three different types of tuna fish; salmon mayonnaise; tiny herrings in a very pungent sauce; small pickled trout; anchovies; shrimp salad; lobster with mayonnaise, and several other delicious sea foods.

Each particular food was distinctive in its own right and each had been perfectly prepared with just the proper seasonings and the most delightfully subtle blendings of herbs. It was a luxurious service and one long to remember.

On the other hand, I can recall being offered hors d'oeuvre at small inns in France and receiving perhaps simply a bowl of fresh radishes still fragrant with that pungent smell of the earth which clings to fresh vegetables, a few green onions, and perhaps a slice of home-cured, boiled ham. This in its way was as thoroughly satisfying and as delicious as the elaborate service in the big restaurant. Both performed their mission in creating a satisfying prelude to a meal.

Naturally, very few homes could possibly serve a tremendous and elaborate hors d'oeuvre service comparable to those in the great restaurants, but it is easy to prepare a tray or two of choice delicacies which will form a most satisfactory first course and create much more interest than the usual first courses served. I have not a grain of respect for the hostess who serves a fruit cup repeatedly as an hors d'oeuvre and doesn't even make the fruit cup interesting enough to be exciting. (And I have had plenty such cups in my experience.)

In case you may want to go completely Continental in your service, I shall outline several combinations of what I term "Table Hors d'Oeuvre." You may arrange this type of first course on a large tray and have it passed at the table, or you may arrange the various foods in attractive dishes and have them tastefully arrayed on a buffet in the dining room with plates and serving tools for the service there. The guests may help themselves and then carry their plates to the tables.

I am listing below possibilities for the home table. Choose your own combinations.

MEATS

A plate of thinly sliced sausages, if the good imported ones are available; or some of the American versions of the European types.

Paper-thin slices of *prosciutto* or Italian ham.

Slices of fine boiled ham or tongue.

Pâté de foie gras or a domestic liver pâté or mousse. There are several American firms now marketing their own pâtés and some of these are excellent.

Special cold meats from a fine-food shop, such as *pâté en croûte,* that is, a highly spiced meat in a blanket of rich pastry.

FISH

Any of the many types of sardines. (Leave them in the can if you can remove the top cleanly and completely, for they will look better this way and are easier to remove singly.) There are large and small sardines in olive oil, mustard sauce, tomato sauce, and with the addition of various herbs and spices.

Anchovies in all their varied forms. (And don't forget the recipe for Jeanne's anchovies given in the earlier section on fish hors d'oeuvre.)

There are at least a dozen different types of herring on the market, prepared for this service, some in oil, some in a marinade, some rolled with other tidbits, and some as fillets in sauce.

Fine tuna fish in olive oil and the tuna fish prepared with herbs and spices.

Smoked salmon and kippered salmon, if you are fortunate enough to be in a part of the country where this is available.

Smoked sturgeon.

Kippered codfish.

Smoked oysters and pickled oysters.

Fresh salmon masked with mayonnaise, with proper accompaniments such as cucumber slices, stuffed tomatoes, etc.

Any of the fish mousses.

Shrimp with mayonnaise.

Lobster with mayonnaise.

Crab legs well arranged on a bed of lettuce or parsley and served with any type of sauce you may prefer.

Individual aspics of fish or shellfish.

Small fish salads.

VEGETABLES

Here I shall mention two sauces repeatedly—"vinaigrette" is one of them. It is made of two or three parts olive oil to one part tarragon or wine vinegar and is combined with as many herbs and seasonings as you may care to use (any of the green herbs, chopped fine, quantities of chopped parsley). Chopped onion, green pepper, celery, and fennel are all good additions to this sauce.

If I say *à la grecque* I mean that the vegetable, which has been parboiled, or not, is cooked very slowly in a sauce made from one pint of water, one third of a pint of olive oil, one teaspoonful of salt, with pepper, coriander seeds, cumin seeds, thyme, parsley, chives, and tarragon. Cook these together for five minutes, adding the juice of one lemon about two minutes before removing from the heat. Poach vegetables in this sauce for varying lengths of time, according to the vegetable, but usually from ten to eighteen minutes.

Tiny artichokes parboiled ten minutes, then cooked in the sauce *grecque* for about fifteen minutes, then chilled.

Stuffed artichokes, parboiled ten minutes, then cooked in the sauce *grecque* for about fifteen minutes. Chilled.

Peeled cucumbers sliced thin in a vinaigrette sauce.

Celery hearts, parboiled for ten minutes, and poached in sauce *grecque* for ten minutes.

Celery root, poached in white wine for thirty to forty minutes, depending on the size, and cubed, in a vinaigrette sauce.

Finocchio, or fennel, parboiled for ten minutes and quartered, poached in a sauce *grecque* for fifteen minutes.

Cole slaw made from both red and green cabbage.

Tiny carrots or matchlike strips of carrot, boiled till tender and covered with vinaigrette sauce.

Cauliflower buds prepared *à la grecque;* cooking time about twenty minutes.

Cold cauliflower buds with mayonnaise.

Tiny onions parboiled five minutes and poached in sauce *grecque* for ten minutes.

Leeks done the same way.

Green onions prepared the same way.

Mushrooms parboiled three minutes and cooked in a sauce *grecque* for ten minutes.

Beets pickled according to your own favorite recipe.

Any of the raw vegetables described in the cold hors d'oeuvre chapter.

Small green peas cooked for about twenty minutes and covered with sauce vinaigrette.

Mixed cooked vegetables with a very tart mayonnaise.

Potato salad.

CHEESE

A cheese tray as described in the section on cheese is acceptable as cold hors d'oeuvre, but not usual, because of the intensity of the flavor and the substantial qualities of cheese.

SALADS

Salads of all types of seafood or vegetables may be served with other hors d'oeuvre; and tiny tomatoes and cucumber boats may be stuffed with a salad for this course.

EGGS

Stuffed eggs of all sorts are most popular for this use.
Eggs in a vinaigrette sauce.
Cold, hard-poached eggs with lobster or shrimp and mayonnaise. (Place the egg on a slice of tomato, top with the shellfish of your choice, and then top with mayonnaise.)
Halves of hard-boiled eggs in a spicy herb mayonnaise.

Condiments of all sorts, pickles, olives, and other accessories of your own invention are good company for the cold hors d'oeuvre tray or table.

It is wise to have not more than six or eight main dishes for the cold hors d'oeuvre service at home, accompanied by several accessories. Here are three suggested combinations to guide you:

Stuffed artichoke bottoms *à la grecque*	Sliced salami
Asparagus vinaigrette	Raw radishes, celery, onions
Shrimps in mayonnaise	Sardines in oil
Chive balls	Anchovy fillets

Cauliflower *à la grecque*	Eggplant *à la grecque*
Soused herrings	Lobster mayonnaise
Brioche en surprise	Stuffed eggs
Raw fennel, radishes, carrots	Parma ham

Olives, pickles, melon rind

Pâté de foie gras	Potato salad
Leeks *à la grecque*	Pickled beets
Crab legs, mayonnaise	Cauliflower vinaigrette
Kippered salmon	Sardines in mustard sauce
Radishes	Head cheese

Olives, celery

Have thinly sliced, dark breads, two or three varieties, crusty French or Italian bread, crackers and biscuits, or hot toast to serve with these and plenty of sweet butter.

If you wish, you may make a more elaborate selection and include several cold meats and use one of these groups with a wine, and coffee later, as the entire luncheon.

Hot hors d'oeuvre service is attractive to many people. In preceding chapters you have many appropriate recipes to choose from. Make your combinations to suit your own taste, either as first courses for luncheon or dinner, or as an entire luncheon.

CHAPTER 8

STOCKING THE LARDER

MY FINAL BIT OF ADVICE TO YOU is about the pantry shelf.
It is all very well to have carefully thought-out and bountiful cocktail parties, but the person who is fortified against
the "drop in" guest achieves the distinction of exceptional
hospitality.

There are a number of standard things it is well to have
on hand at all times—these I shall list later—and which
combine with the staple things always found in the refrigerator—the butter, eggs, cream, and parsley, and the standard condiments of any household.

Each year more and more American firms are becoming

interested in fine foods and taking pains in developing products as distinctive as the formerly imported ones. For instance, the olive growers of California are constantly experimenting and have brought forth a number of excellent new types of ripe and green ripe olives. The sardine packers have been producing packs which compare favorably with some of the foreign ones. There are really delicious boneless and skinless sardines now available through American packers.

Excellent canned shrimp, lobster, and crabmeat are on the market from several different parts of the country. The small Alaska shrimp, which to me has no equal, and the Dungeness crab from the Northwest are worth trying.

You will find excellent American cheese, too, for the producers have been making tremendous strides in perfecting varieties which appeal to the connoisseur. Wisconsin, Oregon, Washington, California, and New York states are only a few of the places where truly great cheese is being produced. The challenge of the European producers finally made many of the domestic cheese makers aware of the possibilities here at home.

I have already mentioned the advance in the baking industry in this country and mentioned the excellence of some of the American biscuits and crackers. Each week sees some new, entertaining product come to market.

Smoked and cured meats in great profusion are to be found in this country, too. They have to be good, for they are aimed primarily at the large foreign groups now living here who still love the national dishes of their homeland

and who demand the best in flavor and quality. Salami, cervelat, *metwurst,* liverwurst and other highly seasoned sausages await you in nearly every delicatessen store. The tiny tenderloins of pork called *Lachsschinken,* which are a valuable aid in the preparation of hors d'oeuvre and canapés are available from Milwaukee, where a great many of these "foreign" products are made. *Prosciutto,* that perennial favorite with the Italians, is produced in this country with the same delicious flavor which made the imported products so very popular.

We have everything in this country to satisfy the gourmet, and I feel that if the producers and the manufacturers continue to find that there is a real demand for the highest quality goods they will make even greater strides. It is up to you and me to create that demand by trying new products and giving constructive criticism. If you feel that a product does not live up to a certain standard, go to the dealer or write the producer and tell him your opinion; give him definite ideas for the improvement of the product. In that way you help promote high quality and specialization.

If you are in a small community where specialty shops are not available, you will find it simple to shop by mail. Most of the great deparment stores throughout the country have pantry-shelf or gourmet shops now, which are well stocked with choice foods; they will be only too glad to keep you informed of their new additions and to do your shopping for you. The large specialty shops in New York and on the West Coast are always anxious to have out-of-town trade and will send you complete lists of their products at any time. Ask several of them to put you on their mailing list.

Here are suggestions for your larder: a dozen cans of sardines in various sauces; a dozen cans of other smoked fish—oysters, smoked salmon slices, anchovies, herring; several cans of other fish—shrimp, lobster, crabmeat, tuna fish in olive oil, shad roe.

Meats: a dozen cans of various meats and pastes; ham, tongue, thinly sliced smoked turkey, for instance. Sausages and mushrooms are always useful too.

Relishes and condiments are necessary and may be kept in any quantity for they are essential at all times.

Always have two or three types of biscuits and crackers on hand, but don't keep them too long.

A few nuts in vacuum-packed containers are always a help when a quick snack is needed.

With the usual things in your refrigerator and some of these pantry supplies you can always prepare one or two canapés or hors d'oeuvre at a moment's notice and know that you are able to extend true hospitality to any guest, unexpected or not.

Fill your party shelf as regularly as you do your staple shelf, for both are important to a well-run household. Never be caught short—with a guest in the drawing room, or on the porch.

Good food and drink are important to good living, but the savour of hospitality and friendship are the most important ingredients. Remember this and you will sail smoothly along in your parties, whether they are large or small, planned in advance or impromptu. The spirit is the thing!

INDEX

Allumettes, 127, 136-137
  Anchovy, 136
  Cheese, 136
  Chicken, 137
  Chicken and Ham, 136
Anchovied Chicken Liver
  Canapés, 134
Anchovies, Jeanne's, 46
Anchovy
  Allumettes, 136
  Brioche en Surprise, 101
  Butter, Nos. 1 and 2, 80
  Cheese Fingers, 131
  Eggs, 50
  and Mushroom Barquettes, 139
  Spread, Nos. 1 and 2, 85
  Tomato Canapés, 95
  Veal Toasts, 96
Antipasto, xiii
Argenteuil Canapés, 99
Artichoke Buds, Stuffed, 59

Artichokes, Fillings for, 60
Asparagus Purée, 106
Asparagus Tip Canapés, 131
Aspic for Fish, 43
Aspics, Individual, 42-44
Aunt Lizzie's Bacon Tart, 159
Avocado
  Eggs, 54
  Filling for Choux, 105
  Open Face, 120

Bacon
  and Cheese Barquettes, 141
  and Hazelnut Sandwich, 125
  Tart, Aunt Lizzie's, 159
Bar equipment for cocktail
  parties, 10-11
Barquettes, 78, 127, 137-141
  Anchovy and Mushroom, 139
  Bacon and Cheese, 141
  Clam, 139

Crabmeat, 140
Crawfish, 140
Curried Chicken, 137
Ham, 140
Lamb Kidney, 138
Lobster, 138
Shrimp, 141
Béchamel Sauce, Basic, 129
Béchamel Sauce for Croquettes, 149
Beef
with Anchovy, 23
Beefsteak en Brochette, 162
Chipped, Spread, 86
Cocktail Hamburgers, 121
Corned, Balls, 152
Croquettes, 151
Paste, Raw, 107
Roast Beef Open Face, 119
Rolls Chinoise, 22
Rolls with Pâté, 21
Spread, 91
Beets, Stuffed, 60
Beignets, 127, 142-145
Biscuit Bases, 74
Biscuits, 178
Bloody Mary, 18
Bologna with Cheese, 29
Bouchées, 77, 127, 145-147
Fillings for, list of, 145
Scallop, 147
Sweetbread, 146
Brazilian Canapés, 97
Brazil Nut Chips, Salted, 174
Bread Bases, 73
Bread Rings, Stuffed, 102-104
Breads for Sandwiches, 109
Brioche, 75
en Surprise, 100
Stuffed, 101

Brochettes, 127
Bronx, 14
Buffet Supper ideas, 180-181
Butters, 79 and ff.
Anchovy, Nos. 1 and 2, 80
Chutney, 80
Curry, 83
Fines Herbes, 79
Fines Herbes, for Veal, 24
Garlic, 82
Horse-radish, 83
Lobster, Nos. 1 and 2, 81
Mint, for Cold Roast Lamb, 25
Mushroom, 83
Mustard, 84
Pepper, 82
Pickle-and-Olive, for Forcemeat, 31
Piquant, 84
Roquefort, 80
Sardine, 82
Shrimp, 81
Smoked Salmon, 81
Sturgeon, 82
Tomato, 83

Canapé, xii
Foundations, 73 and ff.
Canapés, 72 and ff., 95 and ff.
Anchovy Tomato, 95
Anchovy Veal Toasts, 96
Argenteuil, 99
Brazilian, 97
with Brioche, 100-101
Cheese and Ham, 98
Chicken and Almond, 97
Chinese, 98
Danish, 97
Gruyère, 99
Gruyère and Ham, 99

Harlequin, 97
Lobster, 98
Red Caviar, 98
Roquefort, 96
Salami, 100
Sardine, 96
Sardine and Egg, 96
Shrimp, 95
Canapés, Hot, 129 and ff.
    Anchovied Chicken Liver, 134
    Anchovy Cheese Fingers, 131
    Asparagus Tip, 131
    Chicken and Almond, 131
    Chicken Giblet, 134
    Crabmeat, Nos. 1 and 2, 135
    Curried Shrimp, 133
    Egg and Sardine, 133
    Escargot, 132
    Ham, 130
    Ham and Cheese, 132
    Ham and Olive, 130
    Ham and Sardine, 133
    Italian, 135
    Sardine, 130
    Shrimp, 132
Caviar, 46-48
Caviar, Red, Canapés, 98
Celery Root Salpicon, 106
Cheese
    Allumettes, 136
    and Anchovy Paste, 89
    Croquettes, 153
    Eggs, 53
    First Course, 190
    and Ham Canapés, 98
    Hors d'Oeuvre, 33 and ff.
    List of varieties, 34-35
    Mixtures for Dunking, 38-39
    Puffs, 168
    Rolls, Toasted, 123

    Tartlets No. 1, 158
    Tartlets No. 2, 159
Cheese Balls
    Chive, 36
    Curried, 36
    Mexican, 37
    Olive, 36
    Roquefort, 38
    Swiss, 37
Chicken
    Allumettes, 137
    and Almond Canapés, 97, 131
    Barquettes, Curried, 137
    and Cheese Spread, 90
    Croquettes, 148
    Eggs, 54
    Filling, Curried, 103
    Giblet Canapés, 134
    Giblet Sandwiches, 122
    and Ham Allumettes, 136
    and Ham Open Face, 116
    Hamburgers, 123
    Marron Spread, 94
    and Mushroom Croquettes,
        149
    Paste, Curried, 93
    Rolls, 25
    Rolls with Tongue, 26
    Salad for Shells, 32
    Sandwich Open Face, 116
    Spread, Nos. 1, 2, 3, 4, and 5,
        92-93
    and Tomato Open Face, 120
Chicken Livers en Brochette, 163
China and silver for cocktail
        parties, 11-12
Chinese Canapés, 98
Chinese Roast Duck, 33
Chinese Roast Pork with
        Mustard, 33

Chipped Beef Spread, 86
Chive Balls, 36
Choux, Tiny, 104 and ff.
Chutney Butter, 80
Chutney Mayonnaise, 58
Chutney Spread, 85
Citrus Plate, 67
Clam Barquettes, 139
Clam Croquettes, 150
Cocktail Crêpes, 170
Cocktail Hamburgers, 121
Cocktail Sandwiches, 108 and ff.
Cocktails, list of, 13 and ff.
Coconut Chips, 179
Codfish Croquettes, 151
Corned Beef Balls, 152
Crabmeat
    Barquettes, 140
    Canapés Nos. 1 and 2, 135
    Rolls, 167
    Spread, 90
Cracker Bases, 74
Crackers, 178
Crawfish Barquettes, 140
Cream Cheese and Pistachio
    Filling, 102
Cream Cheese Rolls, 124
Crêpes, 127
Crêpes, Cocktail, 170
    Fillings for, list of, 171
Croque Monsieur with Brioche,
    170
Croquettes, 148-153
    Béchamel Sauce for, 149
    Beef, 151
    Cheese, 153
    Chicken, 148
    Chicken and Mushroom, 149
    Clam, 150
    Codfish, 151

Corned Beef Balls, 152
    Ham, 152
    Lobster, 149
    Marron, 150
Cucumber
    Open Face, 119
    Rings, Crisp, 60
    Rings, Fillings for, list of, 61
    Salpicon, 105
    Spread, 86
Curried Cheese Balls, 36
Curried Chicken
    Barquettes, 137
    Filling, 103
    Paste, 93
Curried Eggs, 51
Curried Eggs, Variations, 52
Curried Shrimp Canapés, 133
Curry Butter, 83
Curry of Fruits, 70
Curry Mayonnaise, 58

Daiquiri, 14
Danish Canapés, 97
Danish Ham Rolls, 21
Dark Rum Cocktail, 15
Deviled Eggs, 50
Dill Pickles, Stuffed, 63
Don'ts for cocktail parties, 2-3
Dos for cocktail parties, 3-7
Dressings
    French, 57
    Roquefort I, 57
    Roquefort II, 58
    Russian, 58
Duck, Chinese Roast, 33
Duck Salad for Shells, 32

Egg, Eggs
    Anchovy, 50

Avocado, 54
Cheese, 53
Chicken, 54
Curried, 51
Curried, Variations, 52
Deviled, 50
Fines Herbes, 55
First Course, 191
Fish, 54
Hors d'Oeuvre, 49 and ff.
Open Face, 120
Pâté, 51
and Sardine Canapés, 133
with Sardines, 52
Seafood, 53
Smoked Turkey, 51
Tartar, 53
Virginian, 52
Equipment for making hors
  d'oeuvre, 19-20
Escargot Canapés, 132

Fillings for Bread Rings
Cream Cheese and Pistachio,
  102
Curried Chicken, 103
Ham and Chicken, Variations.
  103
Tartare, 103
Fillings for Choux
Asparagus Purée, 106
Avocado, 105
Celery Root Salpicon, 106
Raw Beef Paste, 107
Salpicon à la Reine, 106
Salpicon de Concombre, 105
Fines Herbes Butter, 79
for Veal, 24
Fines Herbes Eggs, 55

First Course Hors d'Oeuvre, 184
  and ff.
Cheese, 190
Eggs, 191
Fish, list of, 185, 187
French Inn, 186
Meats, list of, 185, 187
Salads, 191
Suggested Combinations, 191
Vegetables, list of, 185, 189
Fish
Aspic for, 43
Brochettes, list of, 45
Broth for Aspics, 43
Eggs, 54
en Brochette, 44-45
First Course, 185, 187
Fritters, list of, 143
Mousse, Individual Molds, 44
Flaky Pastry, 78
Foie Gras Open Face, 116
Forcemeat Sandwich, 31
French Dressing, 57
French Seventy-Fives, 17
Fried Toasts, 74
Fritters, 142-145
Batter, 142
Fish, list of, 143
Meat, list of, 144
Miscellaneous, list of, 144
Poultry, list of, 144
Vegetable, list of, 143
Fruit Hors d'Oeuvre, 64 and ff.
Fruits in Curry Sauce, 70
Fruits Pickled and Spiced, 68

Garlic Butter, 82
Glassware for cocktail parties,
  8-10
Grecque, Sauce, à la, 189

Green Mayonnaise, 40
Gruyère Canapés, 99
Gruyère and Ham Canapés, 99

Ham
Barquettes, 140
Canapés, 130
and Cheese Canapés, 132
and Chicken Spread, 88
Chopped, Open Face, 119
Croquettes, 152
and Egg Open Face, 117
with Melon, 69
and Olive Canapés, 130
Rolls, Danish, 21
and Sardine Canapés, 133
Spread, Nos. 1, 2, 3, 4, 5, and 6, 87-88
Tarts, 160
and Tongue Spread, 88
Hamburger Balls, 166
Harlequin Canapés, 97
Hazelnut Spread, 95
Highball Sandwich, 113
Hors d'Oeuvre, xii
Cold, 19 and ff.
as First Course, 184 and ff.
Hot, 126 and ff.
Hors d'Oeuvre en Brochette, 161-163
Beefsteak, 162
Chicken Livers, 163
Kidney and Lamb, 162
Kidneys and Mushrooms, 163
Seafood, 163
Shish Kebab for Cocktails, 162
Horse-radish Butter, 83

Italian Canapés, 135

Jack Rose, 17
Jeanne's Anchovies, 46

Kibbi, 165
Kidney and Lamb en Brochette, 162
Kidneys and Mushrooms en Brochette, 163

Lamb
Kibbi, 165
Kidney Barquettes, 138
Slices Piquant, 25
Larder Suggestions, 196
Linens for cocktail parties, 11
Liver Paste Open Face, 117
Liver Strudel Rolls, 164
Lobster
Barquettes, 138
Butter, Nos. 1 and 2, 81
Canapés, 98
Croquettes, 149
Mayonnaise, 40
Spread, 90
Louis Dressing, 40

Manhattan, Dry, 13
Manhattan, Standard, 13
Marron Croquettes, 150
Martini, 1940, 13
Martini, 1961, 13
Mayonnaise
Chutney, 58
Curry, 58
Green, 40
Louis Dressing, 40
Mustard, 59
Rouge, 40
Meat
First Course, 185, 187

Fritters, list of, 144
Hors d'Oeuvre, 21 and ff.
Melba Toast, 73
Melon Mélange, 64
Mexican Cheese Balls, 37
Mint Butter for Cold Roast
    Lamb, 25
Mornay Sauce, 129
Mousse Molds of Fish,
    Individual, 44
Mushroom, Mushrooms
    Butter, 83
    Caps filled with Roquefort, 38
    Sandwich, Hot, 124
    Spread, 89
    Stuffed, Nos. 1 and 2, 169
Mustard Butter, 84
Mustard Mayonnaise, 59
My Favorite Bloody Mary, 18

Nutburger Balls, 166
Nuts, list of, 174
Nuts, Salted, 175

Old Fashioned, 15
Olive Cheese Balls, 36
Olives, 176
Olympia Biscuits, 167
Open-Face Sandwiches, 115 and
    ff.
    Avocado, 120
    Chicken, 116
    Chicken and Ham, 116
    Chicken and Tomato, 120
    Chopped Ham, 119
    Cucumber, 119
    Egg, 120
    Foie Gras, 116
    Ham and Egg, 117
    Liver Paste, 117

Roast Beef, 119
Roquefort, 119
Salami and Chives, 117
Sausage and Cheese, 118
Shrimp, 120
Smoked Salmon, 118
Tomato and Egg, 118
Tongue and Water Cress, 117
Oysters, 48-49
    and Bacon, Broiled, 168
    Fines Herbes, Broiled, 168
    Olympia Biscuits, 167

Parma Ham, Rolls, list of, 30-31
Pasties, Small, 153-155
    Fillings for, list of, 154
Pastry, Flaky, 78
Pâté Eggs, 51
Peggy's Radishes, 63
Pepper Butter, 82
Pepper Slices, 61
Pickle-and-Olive Butter, 31
Pickles, 176
Pineapple, Stuffed, 66
    Stuffings for, list of, 67
Piquant Butter, 84
Piquant Lamb Slices, 25
Piquant Veal Slices, 24
Pork, Chinese Roast, with
    Mustard, 33
Pork Rolls, 26
Potato Chips, 177
Poultry Fritters, list of, 144
Prosciutto, Rolls, list of, 30-31
Puff Paste, 76

Radishes, Peggy's, 63
Red Caviar Canapés, 98
Rillettes de Tours, 94
Rolled Sandwiches, 125

Roquefort
    Butter, 80
    Canapés, 96
    Cheese Balls, 38
    Dressing I, 57
    Dressing II, 58
    Open Face, 119
    Spread, 84
    Spread, Variation, 85
    Russian Dressing, 58

Salads, First Course, 191
Salami
    Canapés, 100
    and Chives Open Face, 117
    with Herbs, 27
    Parmigiana, 28
Salmon Rolls, 41
Salpicon à la Reine, 106
Salpicon of Celery Root, 106
Salpicon de Concombre, 105
Sandwich Fillings, list of, 111-113
Sandwich, Highball, 113
Sandwiches
    with Champagne or Punch, 114
    Cocktail, 108 and ff.
    Open-Face, 115 and ff.
    Rolled, 125
Sandwiches, Hot, 121-125
    Bacon and Hazelnut, 125
    Cheese Rolls, Toasted, 123
    Chicken Giblet, 122
    Chicken Hamburgers, 123
    Cocktail Hamburgers, 121
    Cream Cheese Rolls, 124
    Mushroom, 124
Sardine
    Butter, 82
    Canapés, 96, 130
    and Egg Canapés, 96

Eggs, 52
Sauces
    à la Grecque, 189
    Béchamel, Basic, 129
    Béchamel, for Croquettes, 149
    Mornay, 129
    Vinaigrette, 189
Sausage Balls, 166
Sausage and Cheese Open Face,
    118
Savory, xiv
Scallop Bouchées, 147
Screwdriver, 14
Seafood
    Cold, Sauces for, 39-40
    Eggs, 53
    en Brochette, 163
    Hors d'Oeuvre, 39 and ff.
Shish Kebab for Cocktails, 162
Shrimp
    Barquettes, 141
    Butter, 81
    Canapés, 95, 132
    Curried, Canapés, 133
    Open Face, 120
    Spread, 90
Side Car, 16
Smoked Salmon Butter, 81
Smoked Salmon Open Face, 118
Smoked Turkey Eggs, 51
Smörgåsbord, xiii
Soft Drinks, 182
Sours (Whiskey, Rum or Brandy),
    16
Spreads, 84 and ff.
    Anchovy, Nos. 1 and 2, 85
    Beef, 91
    Cheese and Anchovy Paste, 89
    Chicken, Nos. 1, 2, 3, 4, and 5,
    92-93

Chicken and Cheese, 90
Chicken Marron, 94
Chipped Beef, 86
Chutney, 85
Crabmeat, 90
Cucumber, 86
Curried Chicken Paste, 93
Ham, Nos. 1, 2, 3, 4, 5, and 6,
   87-88
Ham and Chicken, 88
Ham and Tongue, 88
Hazelnut, 95
Lobster, 90
Mushroom, 89
Rillettes de Tours, 94
Roquefort, 84
Roquefort, Variation, 85
Shrimp, 90
Stilton, 85
Swiss Cheese and Egg, 89
Swiss Cheese and Olive, 89
Tongue, 86
Tuna Fish, Nos. 1 and 2, 91
Veal, 91
Stilton Spread, 85
Stinger, 17
Stocking the Larder, 192 and ff.
Strawberries, 66
Strudel Rolls, Liver, 164
Sturgeon Butter, 82
Sweetbread Bouchées, 146
Sweetbreads in Shells, 31
Swiss Cheese
   Balls, 37
   and Egg Spread, 89
   and Olive Spread, 89

Tartar Balls, 29
Tartar Eggs, 53
Tartare Filling, 103

Tartlets, 127, 158-161
   Bacon, Aunt Lizzie's, 159
   Cheese No. 1, 158
   Cheese No. 2, 159
   Ham, 160
Tea Table, 182-183
Toasts, Fried, 74
Tomato Butter, 83
Tomato and Egg Open Face, 118
Tomatoes, Stuffed, 62
Tom Collins, 16
Tongue
   with Asparagus, Nos. 1 and 2,
      23
   Rolls Chinoise, 22
   with Roquefort, 22
   Spread, 86
   and Water Cress Open Face,
      117
Tuna Fish Spread, Nos. 1 and 2,
   91
Turkey Straws, 26
Turnovers, 155-157

Veal Slices, Piquant, 24
Veal Spread, 91
Vegetable, Vegetables
   First Course, 185, 189
   Fritters, list of, 143
   Hors d'Oeuvre, 55 and ff.
   Hors d'Oeuvre, Dressings for,
      57
Vermouth Cassis, 17
Vinaigrette Sauce, 189
Virginian Eggs, 52
Vodkatini, 15

White Satin, 14

Zakuska, xiii